No More
Green Chili

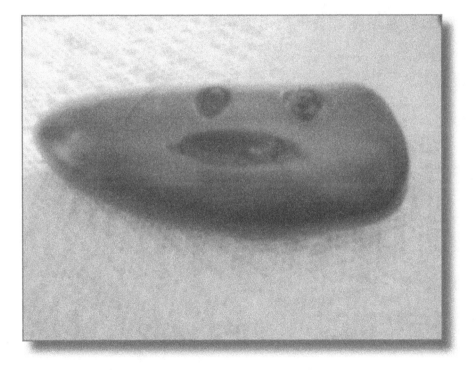

Albert Quintana

authorHOUSE®

AuthorHouse™
1663 Liberty Drive
Bloomington, IN 47403
www.authorhouse.com
Phone: 1-800-839-8640

First published by AuthorHouse 09/27/2011

ISBN: 978-1-4567-2737-6 (sc)
ISBN: 978-1-4567-3021-5 (ebk)
ISBN: 978-1-4567-3022-2 (hc)

Library of Congress Control Number: 2011901235

Printed in the United States of America

Dedication

This book is dedicated to my mom and to all the migrant farm workers who have fed our nation. Their history has been revitalized through this novel, No More Green Chili.

Acknowledgement

Iwould like to thank all the people who made *No More Green Chili* possible. They include all the ancestors of my family, the Chacons and the Durans. Thank you, Aunt Lucy for sharing your life history living as a migrant farm worker. Thank you, Uncle Gene for giving testimony to the hard times,working arduously as a farm worker and also serving as a soldier in World War II. Thank you Mom, for your stories were the most important.

Also, a special thank you to all in the background, Carlos Mora, for his artistry in designing the book cover, Anna Lee Alires, who found all the alabados of Henry Chacon and Beatrice Montoya who translated the alabados.

Table of Contents

Introduction

Not to brag, but I truly believe that my Mother is the best cook in the world, bar none! She has a great heart when it comes to making her best cuisine. Her specialty is green chili. In Spanish it's pronounced chile verde. This homemade chili verde could be the main dish eaten at any given meal, but add a homemade tortilla and a side of frijoles *(beans)* or a side of fried potatoes or maybe mashed; it was a meal to die for. One of my favorite dishes was smothered bean burritos. So anything you added to the green chili was always a feast

The process of making the best dish in world comes quite simply by getting a pound of pork butt and cutting it into small one half inch squares. Then fry the squares until they are golden brown. Using the grease from the fried pork you then brown the flour to make the gravy, add your green chili, preferably jalapenos, diced tomatoes, mexican oregano, cominos, garlic salt, and of course salt and pepper. I can't give it all away because then it would be giving away an old family recipe and that would be taboo.

Making great meals is a learned thing. By this I mean that Mom learned to make green chili from a Mexican woman from Guanajuato, Mexico back in 1960. This is the year that Mom and Dad started a Mexican restaurant business in Denver. The restaurant was called Quintana Roo.

Whoever ate her chili craved more. The neighboring kids would always hang around to see if Mom would roll them a quick burrito and then they would walk away with the biggest smiles.

In 1927 Great Grandfather Francisco Duran visited Henry, Manuelita and the kids prior to Mom's birth. He shared with them a story about a humongous garden that was full of green chili. Within this garden the chili was thriving, growing in abundance. Then one day the chili started dying off. The garden was over taken with weeds and eventually became nonexistent. The metaphor here is that Grandpa Francisco equated the garden to our nation and the people who work, as the chili. When you take the chili out of the garden then your garden is dead. When you take the worker, laborer, bracero, miner, gardener, lumber jack out of our nation, you have nation that is dying. Who built the Great pyramids, The Panama Canal, the Empire State Building, Hoover Dam, and that Golden Gate Bridge? Yes you've guessed it, the Chili Verde of our society.

Have fun reading this book. The stories are real and only reflect a part of your history. We all need a little chili verde in our lives, so enjoy its flavor.

No More Green Chili

By Albert Quintana

Chapter 1

"Like a Thief in the Night..."

Death is consequential, so life its source. No one ever knows exactly when it will come. As one once said, "Like a thief in the night..." Does one live to die? This is something that everyone has to face. It's reality... No one is exempt... One is taught there is an afterlife, something called eternity. But the important phenomenon is what you put between the periods to get to this eternity. There's a beginning and an end, well for this life as much as a human could interpret. This story is about life, a very important life that is the source of my life and others. This life exemplifies meaning, love, dignity and many times human error.

On the evening of Sunday, October 6th 1987, Louise my wife, and I were on our way back from a teacher party in Boulder. It was one of those evenings where it seemed quite routine. My thoughts were one of anticipation. You see, I'm a teacher. On the way home I was already drawing up some lesson plans in my head in preparation for the upcoming week. So on our way home I was very quiet, in deep thought. When we entered our home, the phone rang. It was my brother Mike, he said. "Dad is in the hospital and he isn't doing well, you need to get to Colorado General Hospital, as quickly as possible. He is in terrible shape." Of course my thoughts were he's dead, it always seemed that I always thought, "The worst case scenario." I told Louise that I was going to the hospital alone, but she insisted on going. Desa Rey and Melody my two daughters stayed home with their little brother Javier. I was a mess, couldn't think straight, the only thing that I could think of was Dad dying or already being dead.

Louise drove and insisted that I ride in the passenger seat to the hospital, which was probably a good idea. The messages were clear on the way to the hospital, by this I mean, that I was fore warned of his death. I heard a song on the radio, "The warrior is a child, by Twila Paris" It was as if I was being told that now I was a man and I had the greatest responsibilities in leading my family. I was the warrior in the song. My life would change and now I would take the leadership role.

Hospitals are kind of eerie; there was a scent in the air, it was probably the smell of death. Walking through the hospital to the emergency room was like walking through a fog. The anticipation in seeing Dad's death was in fear. I'll admit I was terrified of death. One year earlier my dog was run over by drunk driver and I lost my composure at the sight of his little mangled body. How would I handle the death of someone I really loved?

As I entered the waiting room, I saw Mom and my brother and sister. The look on their faces was clear that a tragedy had taken place. Mom's first words were, "son, something terrible has happened, your Dad had a massive heart attack and is dead. Go into the next room and say good bye." When I walked into the next room my legs collapsed under my body. I saw his face, his body and the blood stains. All I could do was hold my head to his cold frozen chest and cry unceasingly.

Mom was a very strong woman and was very comforting in always knowing what to say.

"I know that you loved your Dad so much. He is in a better place now."

"You are now the leader of our family, you must be strong."

These words still are engrained in my mind. I really took it to heart when she said that I was the leader of the family.

After our encounter with death, we went to Mom's house. As I entered the front room my two nephews Jose and Lucas rushed me. All I could remember was Lucas holding me so tightly in embrace. I looked down and saw his tiny little hands and arms holding me firmly. His words were, "Grandpa's dead, Grandpa's dead…" beyond a doubt, it had to be the saddest moment in my life. Lucas was 7 years old, just a little kid. His emotion was felt in my heart and the pain was immense. Jose his older brother also held me closely and just seeing the pain in his face was agonizing. Of all the grand children, he was probably the closest to Dad. Jose was like my Dad's little buddy, his tag-a-long, his little dude. The rest of the visit was beyond reason. We sat and cried, reminisced and cried, reflected and cried and cried some more. I'll never forget that night. It will always be etched in my mind.

The drive home was a daze. When we got home Louise gave Melody and Desa Rey the bad news. It was a very sad moment for my baby girls. Javier was too young to have any reaction, but he knew that we were all sad. Melody informed us that, moments after we had left to the hospital, that the front double doors opened up wide, as if a spirit had blown them open. In some beliefs many would say that it was Dad's spirit giving us his last farewell. Melody said that she was so terrified and couldn't sleep. I assured her that it was probably a gust of wind and that there was nothing to worry about. I said, "Just say a prayer and you'll be protected."

Two days later, we were at the viewing. They we were all in attendance, Bernadine my sister, Michael my brother and Mary our Mom. We gathered around Dad's body, held hands and in deep prayer asked God to keep us together as a strong family. We all agreed that this was so important. I'll always remember that covenant that we had in God's presence. You see it was more than a promise, but something sacred, a pledge before God.

Afterwards, we drove to Mom's house and in the drive way was a car. It was Uncle Juan, Dad's older brother and Auntie Lola his younger sister. When I saw them, I ran to them and embraced them so tightly. I tried to hold back the tears, but they flowed profusely.

That night was the Rosary and it was so breathtaking. For years Dad and Mom were part of the Spanish and English church choirs at Our Lady Mother of the Church Commerce City. Music was a big part of our family. Dad played the accordion, guitar and violin and Mom since a young girl would the sing best harmony. This tradition was passed down to us. At that time, Michael had been singing with the Denver Archdiocese Chorale. The chorale group offered their services for all of the Rosary and funeral ceremonies. The music and singing were exquisite. It was like the ceremony for an important political dignitary. As Cousin Tim best put it, "If this funeral would have been in Santa Fe one would of thought that it was the funeral of the governor. The occupancy of the church had surpassed its capacity. People were lined up outside the doors. Everyone knew "Joe Q." Joe Q was my Dad's nick name. His full name was Jose Elijio de la Cruz Quintana. Yes, Dad was a very popular man at Our Lady Mother of the Church and Commerce City. Even though his abuse of alcohol finally caught up to him, he could have a kind and generous side to him. He touched so many hearts.

Just about every friend and relative was there to support the family. The only one not present was his eldest brother. He wasn't able to attend due to the fact that he and his family were branding cattle at the ranch that week. I was very upset and hurt, but life goes on. I just couldn't understand how one could forget one's blood relative in favor of economics. Was the nucleus of the family drifting apart? Was this the beginning of things to come?

At the burial all I could do was think about Mom. How would Mom take on life without Dad? Would her life be better off without Dad? Was it a relief for her now that Dad was not around anymore? His abuse was extreme, when his drinking got out of hand. Did she really mean it when she said that I was now the leader of the family? Who is this woman? Definitely, without a doubt she still is the greatest woman to ever live. She deserves the best. Her roots are deep in culture, if she only knew who she is and where's she's been. She is the most talented woman, the greatest cook! Her smothered green chili burritos were to die for. She was the most talented singer, which was never discovered. All the neighborhood kids would attest that she was the best story-teller and boy, could she hit the best pop-ups flies to prepare me for the baseball season.

Her name is Maria Candelaria Chacon, a.k.a. Lala and Mary. At birth, her father Henry Chacon predicted that she would have the most beautiful voice. When he presented his new baby daughter to his sons and daughters in Spanish, he said, "*Siguiéremos adelante con una vos así claro el nombre de su hermanita es Maria Candelaria.*"

In the American public school system she was known as Mary Candelaria Chacon. She is my Mother, the focal point of our family. She is the heart, the spark of our existence. But the strangest thing is that she never saw herself in that light. She would never take the leadership role and saw herself as a good soldier doing what was told of her. Obedience was taught to her and she did it with total humility. Yet to this day I admire, trust, love and idolize this woman. Once more I say, "Who is this woman?"

At that very instant I could visualize Mom's history, where she lived, her experiences, great grandparents, parents, brothers, sisters, children and everything that made up who she was and is and what her future would be. It was a revelation. It's our legacy!

Chapter 2

Folklore

Legends are passed on from generation to generation. It's called oral history. Will the stories of old die out? Who will tell them? How will they be passed down?

Nestled in the mountains in south central Colorado lived a very special group of people. On their Native indigenous side, their history predated Plymouth Rock over 2000 years and on their Spanish side over 150 years. They were very proud people brought here on pure survival, people who had a strong conviction, devotion and humility for God. Hope was the motivating force to overcome all obstacles in their path. Migration brought them to the Holy Land called Weston, Colorado from Taos, New Mexico. They were a people on the go. Nomadic urgency was in their blood but they also could settle down and create the most from the land. These people were our ancestors.

"Eduardo, mira las mountains, la sierra, que fantástica!" Eduardo, look at those mountains, the Spanish Peaks, they are fantastic." Exclaimed Henry! "They are so pristine in their beauty." We have the best and most beautiful place to live and the best trabajo."

In the distance were the Spanish Peaks also known as the Huajatolla of southern Colorado. The Spanish Peaks-Trinidad area in Southern Central Colorado is an immense area of terrain that changes, surrounding several hundred square miles. It ranges from a semi-arid "desert like" landscape in the lower elevations, all the way to mountainous ski slope terrain in the higher elevations.

There they stood Henry and Eduardo, the Chacon Brothers. Henry and Eduardo were sheep herders in the Spanish Peaks area of South Central Colorado near present day Trinidad, Colorado. They were on their way to the local town of Weston near Trinidad where their parents lived. Payday was in two days and Henry and Eduardo talked about how they were going to spend their hard earned money.

"The first thing that I want to do is go into Trinidad and buy me one of those fancy baths, you know, los banos with bubbles and a nice shave from one of those barbers." said Eduardo. "It's been two months since we had a good bano."

"P U, please Eduardo, face downwind because you smell something fierce," teased Henry.

"Andale Ed, you know we are going to have to give our hard earned money to La Mama," said Henry. "And by the way you don't even shave yet."

"Hey Henry, isn't about time that you find a mamacita yourself?" asked Eduardo jokingly.

At that time Henry Chacon was 19 years old. In his day he made many a young girl turn her head, but still he didn't find that woman that would fit his liken'.

There they stood so proud and robust, Henry with his tobacco pouch in his front shirt pocket, a harmonica in his side satchel and a rifle over his left shoulder. Eduardo also sported a rifle, he was 5 years younger than his brother and he idolized everything Henry stood for. The majority of their supplies were on their faithful mule Adelita. With 200 sheep at their responsibility, the Chacon brothers made their way to the railroad station where the sheep would be taken off to be slaughtered. Also, along on the trip was their loyal Sheppard dog Lelo. Lelo was a mixed breed Border collie and Australian Shepherd mix. He was the perfect sheep dog, the smartest dog in the territory. He protected the sheep with all his wit and instinct and made sure that not one would go astray.

"One more day *Enrique* (Henry) and we will be at the railroad station in Trinidad and then payday!!!" Shouted Eduardo!

"Settle down little *hermanito* (little brother) we will make it in due time, but one more night here in la sierra and down the mountain into Trinidad," assured Henry.

"The night will be here in a few hours, so let's bring the sheep in and set up camp for the night," directed Henry.

The task of setting up camp was an arduous one. Lelo did most of the hard work. Ed whistled as loud as he could and made a circling motion with his hand and then Lelo sped off to work. In minutes, the sheep were all settled in. In the meantime, Henry was making the *cena,* (supper) fresh tortillas and frijoles (beans) and a side of chili pequin and to top the meal off, a freshly brewed cup of coffee.

The young men were extremely tired and wanted to turn in for the night early. Henry was like a usual minstrel, making up lyrics to songs, it was kind of his hobby.

"Jim crack corn and I don't care. Jim crack corn and I don't care. Jim crack corn and I don't care, my master's gone away," sang Henry.

Henry played the harmonica and sang all kinds of variations of songs, in Spanish and in English. He dabbled in the lyrics of many songs quite often, and was also able to sing and write songs for weddings, anniversaries, baptisms, birthdays and just about any occasion. Henry pulled out his harmonica and would blow out a tune. Eduardo was relaxed in his sleeping bag and would hum along to these tunes.

By this time it was dark. The campfire was at its peak, full of reds, yellows and blues.

"You know Henry we've been out here for quite awhile. I sure miss Mom's comida," said Eduardo.

There was a long pause when suddenly a shrill echo came from the mountain top. Lelo started barking unceasingly. Henry jumped up and grabbed his trenta/trenta 30/30 rifle. Eduardo looked as pale as a ghost and said, "What, what, what could that be, que, que, que, es?"

"Calmate mi hermanito, calm down little brother," Henry said nervously. "It's probably a *tecolote,* an owl in an early night kill." "La Virgen will protect us," confidently said Henry.

Moments later a distinct sound could be heard in the distance. Ta-ta, Ta-ta –ta-ta… mama… Ta –ta- ta, mama… mama… Ta-ta-ta- MAMA! Then there was the faint sound, of a horses' gallop in the background.

When Lelo heard this bizarre sound, his two ears propped up and he continued barking, but now he started howling like a coyote. Henry and Ed were scared out of their wits. Finally the eerie sound stopped and the young men had to settle down the sheep. After about 10 minutes, the sheep were settled down. Henry and Eduardo were both in their sleeping bags, but now the Rosaries came out.

"Santa Maria Purisima," stammered Ed. Then Henry continued the prayer, "Santa Maria Madre de Dios, Hail Mary full of Grace… Oh please God be with us and protect us."

The night was still for a few moments when a distinctive shriek clamored through the canyon and echoed for at least five minutes, so it seemed. Ed shouted out, "Get los rifles! Andale Hermano!" Lelo started his howling and then suddenly the whole camp went chaotic. The dishes were scattered all over the ground. Ed went into a frenzy shooting the rifle round after round.

"Stop it Ed you'll run out of ammo!" exclaimed Henry. We need to settle down and see what's going on. The sheep will scatter so quit it!"

Again it took some time to settle the sheep down. And anywhere you looked you expected someone or something to jump out of nowhere. Henry first thoughts were of the old traditional *leyenda* (legend of *La Llorrona*,) the weeping woman. Or maybe someone decides to come up here to pull a joke on us. Not funny! Too scary! Too scary!

At that very instant the sound came back. Ta-ta-ta, ma-ma… Gallop, gallop, gallop… Ta -Ta –Ta- mama "It sounds like a baby calling out for its mother!" Cries out Ed. Ta-ta-ta, mama, mama, mama!! MAMA!! MAMA!! MAMA!! MAMA!! MAMA!!MAMA!! MAMA!!MAMA!! The sound became louder and louder to the point of being thunderous and in an instant through the camp fire flew a white owl and close behind came a horse running at full speed carrying a headless baby in its saddle. All they could do was stare in astonishment… Then the owl circled back and swooped down and barely missed Henry's head. Henry ducked and screamed out, "SANTA MARIA MADRE DE DIOS!"

About 5 minutes had passed and neither Henry nor Ed muttered a word. Then Lelo crawled out from under Ed's sleeping bag. Henry and Ed dropped to their knees and prayed the Rosary until the sun came up. It wasn't until the camp was cleaned up and the sheep were back in order, that the young men talked about the owl and headless horseman or would it is more proper to say headless baby. Oddly enough, Henry found a silver comb stained with blood. Ed said, "I wonder how this got here, it sure is a pretty hair ornament."

Henry told Ed that it would be better if they kept this little secret to themselves. Probably, no one would believe them.

"Say Henry, now we can get into town and get paid," Ed said excitedly.

At the entry point into the town of Trinidad, Henry and Eduardo walked their sheep to the freight train station. At the railroad station, they were met by Tom McGraw the Sheep owner. He was very satisfied with the Chacon brother's accomplishment. The young men were paid for their time in the mountains. Nearby the freight engineer over heard the transaction that took place between the Chacon Brothers and Tom McGraw. The train engineer was so impressed with Henry and Eduardo.

"Say boys, did you run into problems on the mountaintop?" asked the engineer.

"We did not have any major problems. We started with 200 sheep and ended with 200 sheep. As you can see they are a lot fatter and ready for the slaughter house," Exclaimed Henry!

"Well *chicos,* (guys) there are a many sheep herders who come back from the Spanish Peaks area, Huajatolla area, terrified by the evil demons in those mountains," said the railroad engineer. "As the legend says there were two beautiful young girls who went up for the day to the Huajatolla. Their parents asked them to get home before sunset. The real story was that they had planned a rendezvous with their boyfriends. The day was a pretty romantic excursion. Both of the young girls had lost their innocence that day. The legend continues where both of the boys never saw these girls again. Later the eldest of the two found out that she was with child. Her father found out and kicked her out of the house. Not knowing what to do, she walked to the Spanish Peaks in search of her lover. To this day, she is in search of the baby's father. Some people believe that she lost the baby with a late term miscarriage. Some believed that she tried to kill the baby and left the baby to the environment, and others believed that the spirit of the 'Mother's Breasts of Huajatolla raised the baby in the wild. Many sheepherders, who have herded sheep in the Spanish Peaks area, have shared in common that they have heard the cry of a baby." Mama... Mama... Mama... Oh, I forgot to tell you that the Lady had a distinct look about her, she loved to wear silver combs through her hair."

Henry and Ed did not say a word, they were flabbergasted. They both looked at each other, and said, "Maybe next year we should get a different job." Then Eduardo reached into his pocket and found the silver comb that he had found in mountains.

You see in the future, Henry would be my Grandfather. He was born in 1897 in Vigil, Colorado. As a young man he was a sheepherder and tended the sheep and became a miner until he got married to my grandmother Manuelita Duran. Secretively, Grandpa Henry shared this story, only with me. This story was shared because I was persistent and asked too many questions as a young boy. I wanted to know everything about Trinidad, the Spanish Peaks and Huajatolla area. I was able to get a little folklore and secret stories...This man was my Mother's father. She too could tell some most awesome stories, as you soon will find out.

Chapter 3

The Brotherhood

"Am I poor or rich or in the middle somewhere? Can I call myself a believer, a Roman Catholic, a Jew, a Penitente or a Fundamentalist, who am I?"

"Payday, what a nice word to say...Payday," repeated Eduardo. Payday for the Chacons didn't come too often. You see, Henry and Ed were herding sheep throughout the early spring to the beginning of summer. Money wasn't a common thing in those days. People mostly bartered their crops, traded a sheep or two and maybe offered services to their *vecinos*. (Neighbors)

The families in Weston, Vigil, Trinidad and Segundo, Colorado were very religious. The primary religion was Roman Catholic. Mass was given occasionally, maybe once a month by a traveling priest. These priests were from the Franciscan order and were very distinct in appearance. They wore the brownish hooded suits and carried a large wooden Rosary with a huge wooden cross around their waist. Their patron saint was Saint Francis of Assisi. Because the traveling priest was rarely available, the town's people would celebrate their faith through discrete ceremonies and celebrations. Tradition is a big part of the Catholic faith and because the priests were not available, these small communities interpreted their faith in the common with their community.

"Henry, before we go home let's visit Dad's compadre in Weston, Felix Duran. Any way, it's on the way home. He is such a wise man and he tells the best stories about the days of the Indian campaign. You know some people say that he's part Ute," Said Eduardo. "I heard that he has a beautiful daughter named Maria Manuelita. She is kind of short, but she has the most beautiful hazel eyes."

"Come on Henry, you know that you want to meet her!" exclaimed Ed.

Henry didn't say a word, he thought that Ed was acting like your typical younger brother, teasing and talking too much. The two young men walked a mile, when finally they could see the Duran house in the distance. There she was in the back part of the house churning butter.

Then, Henry started to sing a tune. "Oh Eduardo, Eduardo what makes you so fat, a piece of corn bread and a tail of a rat? Oh Eduardo, Eduardo what makes you so fat a piece of corn bread and the tail of a cat?"

At that moment Henry pulled out a harmonica from his satchel and played the same tune. This was a good day for the Chacon brothers, it was payday!

Ed said, "Look, there she is, big brother." Henry said, "Where?" "She's in the back loco, churning butter." Shouted Ed!

"You got to be kidding Ed, for one thing she is very tiny and compadre Felix would never let me talk to her, let alone marry her," said Henry.

Who, said marriage?" asked Ed. "Just meet her!"

Moments later, Henry and Eduardo found themselves at the front door of the Durans. "Con permiso señora, yo quiero hablar con tu esposo, Don Félix." Requested Henry.

Henry was very formal and respectful in his approach, when it came to speaking to his elders. "Entra, pase, jovenes, Don Felix is not here, no esta aqui. He went to the big *junta* (meeting) with the elders of the community. It's supposed to be at a secret place of worship… I believe they are meeting at *la morada* (church) at Segundo," said Dona Duran. "Now that place is on your way home. So be careful and don't let anyone see you," warned Dona Duran. "No one is supposed to go there except the elders," informed Dona Gracia Duran. Your dad should be there, so stay out of sight."

"By the way senora, could we have a cup of water to drink?" asked Ed, as he wiped the sweat from his forehead.

"Better yet I'll make you two growing young men some lunch, said Gracia."

"No, Dona we don't want to inconvenience you," pleaded Henry graciously.

"It's no bother, we were getting ready to eat anyway, plus Manuelita has churned some fresh butter for these fresh tortillas," said Gracia. "Manuelita it's time for the la *cena*. (Supper)"

At that very moment Manuelita walked through the back door. The moment was electric.

"Caballeros, this is my daughter Manuelita," introduced Dona Gracia.

"Good to meet you Manuelita," said Eduardo, "this is my brother Henry and he doesn't have a novia. (Girlfriend)"

"*Callete hermanito*! Be quiet little brother! I apologize for my brother's insolence, Manuelita," said Henry.

At that very moment Manuelita turned toward Henry and gave him the biggest smile imaginable. Henry returned the smile, and then winked at her. Dona Duran noticed this and immediately summoned Manuelita to finish her chores. "Manuelita, you are only 15 years old and are not ready to have a *novio!* (Boyfriend)" scolded, Dona Duran.

"Gracias, Senora Duran, por todo, it was a great meal." The boys said in unison. "We better get going; La Mama Pimenia is waiting for us."

The boys continued on their journey home. "First we'll go to the *morada* (church) and check out this secret meeting in Segundo and then, vamos a la casa..."said Henry.

The boys continued down the hill and approximately 2 miles down the road they could see the morada in sight. The young men were in bewilderment in anticipation of this secret meeting. They were simply clueless. What could these elders of our community be doing, thought the boys? It was approximately 5 pm and the sun was starting its descent. At Segundo, the boys made sure that no one could see them. Henry hid Adelita his mule around to the back of an abandoned house and tied Lelo to a tree some distance from the church. Henry said, "I'll take the first peek and then I'll come back and you can have your view." Then Henry crawled down on his hands and knees to the side window of the church. As Henry got closer to the church, he could hear some sort of singing/chanting going on.

Meanwhile, back at the Duran house, Manuelita was day dreaming about that sweet smile Henry had given her. She thought to herself, that's one very handsome man. I sure hope that I get to see him again. Mama Duran then came to the room and noticed that Manuelita was touched by the experience of meeting Henry. She admonished her daughter and made it clear that she was too young to get involved with this Henry character. All Manuelita could do was listen to her mother. She had great respect for her mother, so all she could do was listen. Dona Duran said, "You know that this Henry character likes to socialize a lot and there are many a young lady, who would love to marry him. So be careful Manuelita, La Virgen will give you a sign and if he's really worthy of marriage, you'll know it. Manuelita said, "Gracias Mama." I'll wait for this sign as I get into deep prayer. "Also mi hijita, Papa' and Juan Chacon are best friends and who knows what those two characters are up to."

After the lecture, Manuelita went back outside and continued her butter churning. Moments later Manuelita's sisters came in and found out that the Chacon brothers were there to visit. The girls heard about the great smile that Henry had given Manuelita.

"Tell us about it Manuelita," said Genoeva. "Well it's simple, Mama introduced us and he smiled. Oh, and I forgot, he also winked at me."

"What was it like Manuelita?" asked Genoeva.

"It's hard to explain, it just made me feel good inside." responded Manuelita.

"Is he handsome?" As Genoeva, continued asking questions.

"You better believe it, he's gorgeous," responded Manuelita with a red face.

"Does he have a brother," asked Aurora?

Mama Duran heard the girls chattering. La Mama Duran came running out the back door and said, "In the Duran tradition we have a saying," "*No manches la bandera*, "Do not stain the flag!' The flag is clean and men do not respect women that have... She retorted and said, "Do I make myself clear?" "

"Si Mamacita you make yourself muy *claro*, real clear!"

Manuelita was the oldest of the girls, next was Aurora, then Genoeva, Jesucita and the youngest Ramona. She had two older brothers, Eduardo and Chencho and the youngest was little Frank. Gracia Duran was very strict with her girls and didn't want any of them to get pregnant. Manuelita had to set the example for her younger sisters. It was so important to make her family proud. The flag was a metaphor for a girl's treasure, her innocence and this flag could not be stained. Dona Gracia was a proud loving and God fearing woman. She was brought up to raise her children to believe in Jesus Christ and the Blessed Virgin. The family's dignity was of utmost importance.

Back at la morada the anticipation was building. Henry looked around and slowly got down on his fours and crawled to the window of the church. To his amazement he saw several men from the community. Juan his dad, Felix, Manuelita's dad and many of his older *primos,* cousins were in attendance. There was a huge 10 foot wooden cross in the middle of the church. One man was chanting an *alabado* (worship song), while another was tied to the cross. The man was not on the cross, but tied to the cross like a whipping post. Another man was whipping the man on the post until he bled. The man being whipped would grunt and at times scream. Then when the man would scream the man whipping would say, "every time you scream like a woman you will get an extra lash." Then the Penitente leader chanted out an alabado and the others would repeat it, repeat and repeat.

"Bendice Señor la cena en la mesa, de altar y hechemos su bendición. Como Padre Celestial..." (Holy Father blesses this meal at your altar and blesses us, heavenly Father, "chanted the leader of the group. *"Este sagrado convite en la mesa del altar, es la cena del Señor en la corte celestial...* (This sacred invitation to the altar is the meal of the Lord in His celestial court... *La bendición de Dios padre hechemos omnipotente en esta Santa morada. Desde cuerpo de tu gente...* Our Father's blessing is omnipotent in this Holy chapel and is the body of Christ...) *Padre Bendice a su pueblo que Te pide contrición en esta Santa morada hechemos su bendición...* (Father blesses your town that asks forgiveness at this Holy chapel. Give us your blessing...) *El jueves Santo en la noche a todos los comulgó Y entre acidentes de pan su cuerpo nos dio...* (On the night of Holy Thursday you gave us your body in the form of bread...) *Y al mismo tiempo les dijo, que había de ser experimentar que en aquella misma noche, todos lo habían de dejar...* (At the same time, He said that the people didn't know what He would go through and that they would abandon Him...) *San Pedro que aquí está ya le cupo un grande pesar. Señor Bendice la cena en la mesa del altar...* (Saint Peter who is here now would share great burden, Holy Father blesses this meal at the altar...) *Con el bello de Jesús le vamos acompañar en la Santa Morada y en La mesa del altar...* (With Christ's beauty we will join Him at the Holy Chapel and at the altar...) *Por las animas, Benditas debemos todos rogar en esta Santa Morada en La Mesa Del altar...* (We the holy should pray in this Holy Chapel at the altar...) *Señor en esta Santa Morada Nos distes el alimento sin merecerlo. Hechemos tu bendición...* (Lord, at this Holy chapel, you give us sustenance even though we are not worthy. Give us your blessing...) *Amen, Gracias Te damos Señor..."* (Amen, we give thanks to you Lord...)

Henry could not believe his eyes. Mi Papa is in there and is being as brutal as an animal, he thought. What were these chants they were singing? This is supposed to be place of worship and Jesus already died for our sins. Why, is this humiliation so barbaric and sinful thought Henry? The chanting became so loud that in the background Eduardo whistled and Henry could barely hear it. The chanting was similar to a powwow of the local Utes who chanted and sang songs around a drum. Henry then remembered it was Eduardo's turn to witness the debacle. Henry then noticed that all of the men would take turns whipping each other at the whipping post. Then after several minutes, Henry made his crawl back to Eduardo.

"*Mi manito*, my little brother, I don't know if it's wise to witness what's going on inside. You will be surprised what you might see," warned Henry.

"Oh brother you know that I can handle it. Remember what happened with the headless baby," reminded Eduardo. "Okay mi *manito*, do it, but be very careful," warned Henry.

After witnessing the mortification, Eduardo came running as fast as he could. "Andale, Enrique the meeting is over, we need to get home before Papacito, whispered Eduardo. Hurry I don't want to be on that whipping post,"

So the frightened young men picked up the pace and arrived at the Chacon residence before Papacito. As they arrived, Henry whistled and Pokey, one of the other dogs of the family came running as fast as she could. Lelo and Pokey were jumping with joy. La Mama Pimenia, Eloisa and Delfinia poked their heads out the screen door and started shouting, "Enrique and Eduardo *estan aqui*, Henry and Ed are home at last!"

Then La Mama Pimenia immediately said, "Your father will soon be here and then we'll all be able to have the *cena*. (Supper)"

"Sons you will have to tell us about everything about *La Sierra*, (Spanish Peaks)" Said, La Mama.

La Mama Pimenia wasn't Enrique's biological mother; actually she was Juan's third wife. Juan lost two wives prior to La Mama Pimenia, due to death while giving birth. The mother of the children was Candelaria, but La Mama was a great step mother to Enrique and Eduardo and their sisters Eloisa and Delfinia.

Don Juan Chacon came in minutes later. He was so happy to see his two sons who made it through the spring with the sheep. Don Juan was a man of few words but because it was a special occasion Juan summoned his wife to bring in the homemade *cerveza*. (Beer) Then they all met in the *cocina* (kitchen) to have the meal.

"Que rica, es la comida. The best cook in the territory." said Eduardo. "I was getting tired of frijoles every day, noon and night."

"Sons did you see anything peculiar in your excursion in the mountains?" asked Don Juan.

"No Papacito," responded the boys.

At that very moment Don Juan asked La Mama Pimenia to go to her bedroom. "We have some serious business to talk about, "man talk," said Juan as he took a swig of the beer.

"Sons, this is very important to me and la familia. Were you at La Morada this evening? Someone spotted two young men running away from the Morada. Chencho said that it looked like you two hombres. Now you better not be, bull shitting me," warned Don Juanito.

The boys sat quietly, while Don Juanito scolded them.

"Now if you were at La Morada in Segundo, it's important that you keep this a secret."

"Why Papa?" asked Eduardo.

"*Por que es muy importante que nadie sabe que nosotros tenemos tradición!*" lectured Juan. We are a proud people who have a great belief in the tradition of the Catholic Church.

"Father what are you trying to tell us?" asked Henry.

"Now it's important that not even my wife know," said Juan. "That's why she is in the kitchen right now."

"I guess it's about time I tell you about my secret life, said Juan hesitantly. "You are men now and it's time that you become part of this secret. En la manana, tomorrow morning I will take you to a secret place and divulge my story… So be prepared for the unexpected."

Later that night, Henry and Eduardo got to bed… "I think that Dad is telling us this story because he knows that we were at the morada, "said Eduardo.

"What could all of this mean? Not to change the subject but, do you think that she'll marry me?" asked Henry.

"Who are you talking about big brother?" asked Ed.

"You know exactly what I'm talking about, Manuelita, stupido! She is the prettiest woman that I have ever seen in my life, a real woman. She will make a great *esposa* (wife). The only thing is, that she is pretty young," said Henry.

"As the old cliché states, wait for a sign from La Virgen," suggested Eduardo.

"Bueno, brother I'll wait for a sign," said Henry…

"Now the other issue is what is going on with Dad?" asked Henry. "Well, tomorrow morning we'll find out. You know that it has something to do with what we saw at La Morada."

The next morning was a very beautiful day. Henry and Eduardo were up early, ate breakfast and were ready to go and find out what this secret life was all about.

"Okay boys it's time to become real men of God!" emphasized Dad.

They made their way to Segundo by horse and buggy and there, they were in La Morada. Papacito pulled out his book of *alabados* (Holy songs) and *La Biblia Santa* (The Holy Bible.)

"You see my sons, we here in Weston and in Trinidad do not have enough direction and guidance from the Holy Roman Catholic Church. Occasionally, we get a Franciscan priest to celebrate La Misa with us. For this reason, we as men have to lead our families in the Tradition of the Holy Roman Catholic Church. We are obligated to evangelize the world as a result of our Baptism. So in order to do this, I must pass on this "Tradition" down to my sons and grandsons," instructed Juan. Juan continued, "I have dedicated my life to the example and self-sacrifice of Jesus in his Passion, and observe all penitential devotions of the Hermandad. Sons, I belong to the Hermandad Piadosa de Nuestro Padre Jesus Nazareno or in English known as, The Pious Brotherhood of Our Father Jesus the Nazarene. It dates back to Spain in the 12th century. In short, I'm a Penitente. I suffer for Jesus Christ in his passion. Many of the men in our community are Penitentes. It is our responsibility to share the water rights of our community, settle disputes and when families are in need, help them. It is truly a brotherhood. We must help one another, as Jesus taught us, to love one another. But the key is in the sacrifice that we share during the Lenten season, the forty days before Good Friday. As you both know that Jesus' Passion is why we do this," explained Juan.

"Padrecito, you talk about a sacrifice, what is this sacrifice?" asked Henry.

"It's the re-enactment of Christ' Passion on the Cross," explained Juan.

"Do you actually crucify someone?" asked Ed.

"In the Catholic Church, we practice a tradition known as mortification," explained Juan. "Mortification comes from the word, muerte or death. We do not kill anyone, but we deny our carnal desires for the forty days. Men must not commit any sin against the Ten Commandments. In addition, we in secrecy, whip one another to constantly remind us what Jesus went through on his way to the cross. Many of our hermanos have been very sinful throughout the year and because a priest is not present for confession and Holy Communion, the denying of one's carnal desires is our penance. During these forty days, men must abstain from adultery, stealing, cheating, and celibacy as a penance. During the ordinary time of the Church we are responsible for leading the communities' rosaries, prayer vigils, wedding ceremonies, and funeral wakes," explained Juan.

"Papa, why is this, such a huge secret?" asked Ed.

"This is a secret organization because of the misunderstanding of the other Catholic orders of priests in the Catholic Church. The Irish Catholic priests frown on our religious practices and other people of our country, who do not have an understanding of our brotherhood. They believe that this tradition of the church is so barbaric and archaic. So, we even keep this secret from our wives and children. Our wives just believe that we are doing the business of the community at these community meetings. They approve of all our confraternity obligations, but the flagellation remains a mystery, my sons. So I'm asking you to become Penitentes as well?" petitioned Juan.

"At this very instant, our beautiful state of Colorado is being infiltrated by European settlers who have come to work in the mines. Felix and I are presently working at the Primero mine and have worked with people from Greece, Italy, Lebanon and other European countries. They do not understand our traditions. So we must hold tight to our *cultura* (culture). Many will come with a new form of Christianity known as Protestantism. They have priests that are married and do not believe in the Holy Eucharist as we do. So be prepared, because they will try to baptize you, but my sons you have been baptized. You have to be strong in your beliefs. Many of these priests who are married will solely believe in the Holy Bible, I tell you we have the Bible also, but the difference is that we have the doctrine that is consistent throughout the world. Generally speaking, their doctrine is in accordance to whoever is preaching. Somos Catolicos! Nada mas! Catolicos!" Juan emphasized proudly.

Henry and Ed were so touched by their dad's speech, then without hesitation they said that they would be proud to be Penitentes.

"Well Papacito, where do we do we sign up?" asked the boys.

"Well sons when you were grazing the sheep in the *sierra* (mountains), I recommended you to Los *Hermanos* (brotherhood). They were all in agreement that you would both be great Penitentes. They thought that Eduardo might be somewhat young, but when they heard that he had spent time in the sierra, they knew that it was time and he was ready," said Juan.

Henry and Eduardo became Penitentes and went through all of the requirements. Manuelita's older *primo* (cousin) Francisco was the Christ that year and went through the reenactment of the Passion. The day was one that will never be forgotten. The ceremony's ritual was based on the Stations of the Cross. There were 14 stations and the Hermandad played out the Passion to the "tee". The beginning part was the most memorable. There was an eerie sound that came from a fife-like reed instrument that they called a pito. Francisco and the Roman soldiers processed down to the first station and then the second station and then flagellation took place. There was blood everywhere. Henry and Eduardo tried to be strong, but tears were rolling down their faces. The young men wiped their tears immediately so that Juan wouldn't see their weakness. The pito continued to play this bizarre sound. Along with the sound of the Pito, the Hermandad sang a series of verses from the alabado of the Passion of Christ. There was a wooden cross erected on a hill north of the Chapel (*Morada)* at Segundo. Francisco was whipped and hung on the cross for a long time, but the elders knew when it was time to bring him down.

After the reenactment of the Passion, the families of the Hermanos all met at the park in Weston and had celebrated Easter with a great fiesta. Felix, Manuelita's dad donated a cow and the barbeque was in the making. Dona Gracia was there and of course, Manuelita and her sisters. Manuelita also had an older brother named Eduardo who was the eldest of the Duran progeny. The Lenten season was over, so the men brought out the homemade beer and then sang songs to the wee hours of the morning. Enrique was the star of the celebration, playing his mouth harp and singing some of the songs of the time. Henry's favorite song was, "It ain't gonna rain no more." All of the young ladies were intrigued by Henry's talent and lyrics. Henry's education was only to the first grade of grammar school, yet he could sing and write, in both Spanish and English. This alone, proved that he was a very talented man.

Gracia, Felix and the rest of the family went home early that night. As Manuelita exited the park, her eyes were set on Henry, and of course, his on her. As the Duran clan were leaving the party, Henry busted out a tune and sang both in Spanish and English, "It ain't gonna rain no more, no more...It ain't gonna rain no more, no more. It ain't gonna rain no more. How in the heck can I wash my neck, if it ain't gonna rain no more?"

It ain't gonna rain no more, no more. It ain't gonna rain no more. So how in the dickens can I water my chickens? If it ain't gonna rain no more, no more."

Chapter 4

The Exodus

Coal fields around the Trinidad area

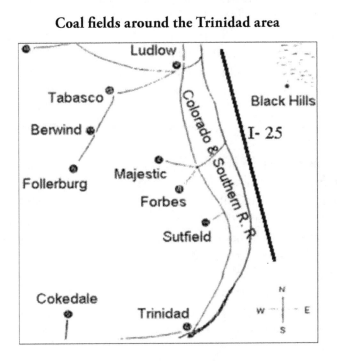

The summer of 1913 was here, and now it was time for the Chacon Brothers to find employment. Both Felix Duran and Juan Chacon were employed by C.F. &I. (Colorado, Fuel and Iron Company.) at the Primero mine, not too far from their homes in Weston. The C.F. &I Coal Company was a very lucrative business in the United States. At its best production, the Primero's mines could produced 3,000 tons of coal a week and employed an average of 600 men. The mines were the main source of income to the people of the surrounding vicinity. (Williams)

Coal was a great resource for many Americans in the early 1900's. Coal could be used as a heating source for homes, but its main use was for the making of steel. Steel was a man made product used primarily for bridges, skyscrapers, trains and the automobile. History tells us that this man- made metal was one of the main causes of the industrialization of the United States.

In 1913-14, miners struck against the mine company and suffered through one of the most severe winters in Colorado history. The Ludlow incident up north, near Walsenburg turned into a massacre where many innocent mine workers and families were killed. The Ludlow Massacre set fear in the people which therefore, set a chain reaction to the exodus of many families who held strong foundational roots in Weston and the surrounding region, which included the Chacons and the Durans.

"There is an old saying, my sons, "that this world is made up of a lot of love and work," said Juan. "I just hope that there is a balance and you don't become a bunch of *huevones!" (Lazy bones)*

"*No te preocupes papacito*, (don't worry father) we will make you proud!" exclaimed Eduardo boldly.

Immediately, on the first day of work in the mines, the Chacon brothers were confronted by Roberto Gallegos, the union representative.

"Men, I'm Roberto Gallegos and I am enlisting young men to be a part of the union. Our union is called the United Miners of America. We are bargaining for an eight-hour day, getting paid twice a month and working in areas in the mine that are properly ventilated. These are demands that are warranted by law, but we want it in unionized literature so that we work in complete safe conditions. So are you in?" asked Roberto.

Juan and Felix were not a part of the union. The boys looked to their father and Juan just said, "We'll let you know at the end of the work day."

When the boys entered the worksite they were immediately separated. Juan went with a group of men and entered mine C, while Eduardo went with Felix into mine F. Henry was on the ground level of the mine and mirrored the foreman delegating the jobs to the other workers. Henry was somewhat apprehensive, but was a great listener while being given instructions. There was a break at the hour and in groups of four, the miners would come up for clean air and for a drink of water.

Henry was the water boy for the first day and thought to himself, this job is pretty easy. As he gave drinks to the workers he wondered when Eduardo would come up. As each miner came up he couldn't recognize the faces. Finally, Eduardo came up and asked for water.

"I want a double," pleaded Eduardo.

Henry said, "Wait until it's your turn."

Henry didn't realize that it was Eduardo.

Finally, Eduardo said, "it's me pendejo, your brother!"

Henry could not recognize Eduardo because his face was so black from the coal soot.

"I'm sorry hermanito, but I couldn't recognize your face. The strange thing is that I did recognize your smell, but I wasn't sure," joked Henry.

"How is it down there?" asked Henry.

"It's kind of scary. You are down there with very little light and you have people drilling the coal from the walls, while the others are shoveling coal into the rail cars which, are powered up to the main level for shipment. We all take turns shoveling and drilling, and boy is it hard work," said Eduardo.

"Is it hard to breath down there?" asked Henry.

"Yes, it is extremely difficult to breath," said Eduardo.

"How did you get the easy job?" asked Eduardo.

"Don't know… I must just have a pretty face," joked Henry.

The day's work lasted 12 hours and at the end of the day the Chacons and Durans joined the United Mine Workers of America. Well, for Henry, his short lived day as a water boy lasted, that one day, and he too went deep into the mines the next day to make a living.

The second day of work had changed for Henry, now it was his turn to go deep into the mine. As Henry's crew was burrowing deep into the earth's surface his thoughts were of a cave in. He started to pray the Rosary silently and asked the Lord for protection. But in his fear he knew that his image would have to be brave and macho. He didn't want the other miners to know that he was scared out of his wits. The underground foreman asked him to be in charge of the first shift of drilling. Henry took the drill and started drilling. This drilling apparatus must have weighed at least a hundred pounds. Henry started drilling and couldn't believe the pain that shot through his arms. The other miners started laughing and knew that this young kid couldn't do this job.

The foreman said, "By the end of this week you will be able to drill like a true veteran. You will be a real man, like Juan your father."

An hour later, Henry fell to the ground from exhaustion. His arms were so sore they were ready to fall off. The foreman gave him 5 minutes to recover and then he was instructed to shovel in the coal into the rail cars that would be elevated for transport to the surface. Shoveling the coal into the cars was also a very grueling job. Finally, it was time to call it quits for the day. When Henry got to the surface, he was blinded by the light. Eduardo was waiting for him and saw Henry as he came out of the mine and couldn't stop laughing.

"Why are you laughing, brother?" asked Henry, angrily.

"You looked so funny when you came up, you looked like a mole trying to find its mother," laughed Eduardo.

After two weeks of this tough, grueling work, the Chacon brothers started to feel their bodies getting stronger and stronger. Occasionally, they would find themselves in arm wrestling contests and of the two young men; Eduardo became quite strong and skillful. Henry always thought of himself as the artist of the family, where Eduardo was the brawn.

One day after work, the brothers decided to go the local joint in Weston to have a drink. Outside the bar was a man reciting poetry in Spanish and English. Henry had written many poems himself and was intrigued by this man's skill. Henry was very observant in learning this man's style. This talented man's delivery style was the use of memorization. He also had written many books, which he had on display. He was a troubadour, a professional writer and poet who traveled from town to town. He could be hired at weddings, funerals and any occasion to give a dedication to the occasion.

After this experience, Henry went home and started to write. Remember, he only had a first grade education. During this time in history the use and delivery of media was very limited, so Henry became a troubadour, a traveling entertainer who would make use of his poetry, songs and *alabados* (Holy Songs). To add to his resume he became a pretty darn good square dancing caller. Many people were coming to the square dances from many diverse backgrounds; it was where one could be, "American."

The barn dances were big on the radio. Henry was able to memorize all of the calls in order to make the square dance a success. He knew his do-si-dos, pass throughs, arm turns, do pasos, dive throughs, cloverleaves, promenades and many more calls. His best calling came when he used the calling style of Ernest Legg, one of the best callers in the nation. Now Ernest was famous because he was calling barn dances on the radio. This cultural trend was spreading like wildfire throughout the nation. "Ladies do and the gents you know, promenade and do- si- do," were Henry's favorite calls. He was well known throughout Las Animas County and went as far north as Walsenburg to show off his skills. There were many young ladies who wanted to be introduced to Henry and who knows, maybe he had a fling or two. Grandpa Henry was so diversified in his talents one would never be surprised at what new skill he'd pick up. He loved to have a lot of fun. Cedric the Entertainer had nothing on Henry Chacon. This was one of Dona Gracia's cautions of Henry; he likes to socialize too much. So with this implanted in Manuelita's head, she was very hesitant in pressing the courting with Henry.

After about a month the job started to wear on the workers. The union and coal company started to negotiate the contract for the next three years. A contract usually was negotiated for a three year period. The company and the coal miners at Primero seemed to have a good working relationship, but up north at the Walsenburg and Ludlow mines there was a lot of dissatisfaction between the coal company and the union.

The winter of 1913 was not a good time for Felix Duran and his family. Felix took some time off of work to be with his wife Gracia. She became very ill. Months prior to her death, she complained about a knot in her lower abdomen. Some people thought that she was *embrujada* (bewitched), but the diagnosis was stomach cancer. Unfortunately, a little after Christmas, the Durans buried their Mother.

At the Rosary, the Hermandad Penitentes chanted and sang the alabados. Henry sang a very special alabado for Gracia.

"Yo quiero dedicado un alabado a La Dona Gracia Valencia Duran, I want to dedicate praise to God for the soul of Gracia Valencia Duran" announced Henry.

Henry sang,

"Ese camino de Dios lo ponen crucificado, hay lo anduvo de rodias
mi Amiga Gracia…

En el calvario la ven en su carreta sentada pidiendo su limosnita
mi amiga
Gracia

Y le reza su sudario en el calvario postrado y le echan mi bendición
mi amiga Gracia…

Los esclavos de Jesús son los que la acompañaban
En su sagrada pasión
mi amiga Gracia…

Este día anduvo en su carreta postrada
Acompañando a Jesús
mi amiga
Gracia…

Y lo suben con cadenas con mi marrada a que los bendiga Dios
mi amiga Gracia…

Jesús, Jesús de mi vida
Ándale los tres vaqueados con una vela en la mano
mi amiga Gracia…

Y la ven martajas el paciente te reclama
Para clavar su cajón
mi amiga Gracia…

El Señor la llama para que lleve aquella alma,
Con su espadita en la mano
mi amiga Gracia…

Dónde va San Juan Bautista con El Señor?
Caminando esperando a sus pacientes que para el cielo
Va guiando…

Donde va El Niño perdido con su túnica morada
Y su corona de espinas y la sangre en sus espalda?

Y a lo llevan por la calle de amargura.
Atado de pies y manos amando a la colona…

Es tan estréchala la cama que tubo
El Hijo del hombre.
Que para morir en ella un pie sobre El harto pone…

El domingo servio al cielo,

Amen Jesús
Le gritaban esta su mama
Con Dios comadre Gracia…
Amen

In translation Henry was telling the people at the services that the life and way of Jesus was hard and that Gracias' life was dedicated to this life. This alabado takes Gracia through a journey, from her burial to the transition into Heaven

The community was so sad to see such a loving lady go to her rest. She displayed the ultimate example to the rest of the people in Weston. The people called her, *La Mujer* (the Woman) because of her involvement with others in the community as a midwife.

"Padrecito, what are we going to do now that Mama is gone?" asked Ramona.

"Well mi *hijita,* my youngest, most beautiful daughter, we will have to do our best as a family. Manuelita, you are my eldest daughter. I'm asking you to be the greatest example to your sisters. My daughters, you are to respect Manuelita, as your own mother, do you understand me," demanded Felix!

"Eduardo and Chencho you are to be great big brothers to your sisters and are responsible for your sisters when I'm not around, do you understand?" shouted Felix. "Do you understand?" Then they broke down crying, embracing one another. The daughters were so hysterical, that poor Felix did not know how to handle the situation. So he brought the whole family together to pray the Holy Rosary.

"Hail Mary full of Grace…" recited Felix. After the rosary the family vowed and made a covenant to God that they would stay close to one another and hold trust in Jesus and La Virgen.

In the next three months, January, February and March of 1914, the Durans and Chacons became very close. La Pimeda Chacon became a part time surrogate parent to the Duran siblings. The Chacons and Durans were very fortunate to own their homes, where the other European immigrants who came to work the mines had to live in company homes and live on scrip. The Chacons and Durans did not have to live on company scrip, where the immigrants owed their souls to the company store. Scrip was a representation of money. When a family was in need of food they would go to the company store and use their scrip to purchase the food items.

The price of food was outrageous and usually a family did not have enough scrip to cover their bill, so the store would give the families credit.

On the morning of April 14th 1914 the Chacons and Durans were confronted by Robert Gallegos. "Sorry my brothers there will be no work today," said Roberto. "There have been some killings at the Ludlow mine. "Presently, we are on strike… The Mine Workers Union has called for a strike… The coal company has hired some professional soldiers to control the union workers. The families have been evicted from their company homes and are now housed by the union in tents. Several union reps have been killed, the whole place is in chaos," said Roberto. "We will have a union meeting this evening to decide what we here at Primero need to do," explained Roberto.

"Roberto, "what do you want from us?" asked Felix.

"Just be at the meeting tonight at the Weston Grange hall at 7 pm," instructed Roberto.

In fear, the Chacons and Durans were so distressed about the Ludlow killings they never went back to the grange. They just wanted to mind their own business and find another way of making a living. The Primero mine stayed closed for some time. Later, many more Europeans came in droves to replace the unionized miners.

Two weeks had passed when an opportunity arose. A man came in from the Colorado Springs area by the name of Jack Wilson. He had been going door to door soliciting workers to come to Fountain and work in the saw mill.

The Advertisement read

Wanted 500 Men to work in the Fountain saw Mill

No Experience needed

Great Opportunities

Apply at the saw mill main office On main street

It wasn't too long after this advertisement and invitation to come to Fountain, Colorado, that the Chacons and the Durans made their way to Fountain, Colorado. The exodus from Weston was a very painful one for the families. The Chacons and Durans were not the only families to migrate to Fountain. There were many other families who made this mass exodus out of the southern Colorado area. There were also many other Hispano families who made their way to northern Colorado to work for the Great Western Sugar Company. Thus, this was the birth of the migrant worker in Colorado.

Chapter 5

The Birth of a Migrant

**Tragedy can cause change.
Why would one want to leave their
homeland and give up their roots?
To do jobs no one else wants to do?**

The year was 1914. The Ludlow Massacre and the death of Gracia were major factors in the move to Fountain. Thus, tragedy caused change.

The Durans' and Chacons' transportation to their new home was not by car or truck, but by wagons pulled by mules and horses. The road to Fountain was not on Interstate 25 or Highway 85 as we know it today, but a very rutty, muddy, dusty and bumpy road. Summer was approaching and the days were getting quite hot, which added to the misery.

Henry was up to his typical upbeat attitude… His harmonica kept everyone entertained. The Duran sisters were very amused by his talent and comical personality.

"Hey ladies how long do you think it will take to get to Fountain, Colorado," asked Henry?

There was no answer from the Duran senoritas, they just sat there and giggled the entire time. It didn't matter what Henry said, he could have said that the sun was blue and they'd go into hysterics laughing. Henry made the pain of leaving Weston a little easier. The girls were still mourning the loss of their mother, so Henry's great personality made the move a little less painful.

"The advertisement said that there will be a lot of *oportunidad* (opportunity) at this place called Fountain," said Felix.

"Our experience in logging pines is lacking somewhat, but with our numbers we should be able to put our strong young men to work," said Juan boastfully! The two Eduardos, Henry and Chencho should supply the hard labor for us to live comfortably in this paradise," continued Juan.

"Yes, this working force is the key to our success, we need to work together as an *equipo*(team) as do the Jews, Serbs and Italians who come into our country," said Felix.

"The girls will all have to find husbands who are great workers. The younger kids will have to go to school and get some basic education," continued Felix. "Compadre we have a lot ahead of us. Who knows, maybe I'll find a good woman who will help me raise these younger kids," said Felix despairingly. "Frank is only 2 years old, so we'll have to raise him together. Just imagine a two year old without a mother, que lastima! What a pity! It just not fair! There is no justice!"

At that very moment Felix' eyes welled up with tears. Juan was a good friend and assured him that all will be well and to have faith that God will come through for us.

"Don't worry compadre we will make a great team…" said Juan. "Tu sabes compadre, you know my friend there will never be another like Gracia, tu Gran Mujer"

"Gracias mi amigo, you are truly a great friend, seguro, you are a great friend," said Felix.

The trip from Weston to Fountain was approximately 138 miles and with the slow beasts of burden pulling the wagons, the Chacons and Durans could only travel 20 miles per day. The trip took 7 days. Imagine the worse vacation you've ever been on. No comfortable seat to rest on like your lush suv, but a wooden seat that would at times give you a splinter or two. No dvd player to see the latest movies. No air conditioning, but a cool breeze running through your hair as the horses would pick up speed. The mode of transportation was either a model A, a horse drawn buggy or a wagon drawn by mules or horses. The travel was dependent upon your economic status. The Chacons and the Durans were very poor, especially now, without home and only a prospective job in Fountain.

The seven days to Fountain were long and drawn out, it seemed like eternity. There were many stops to accommodate the children. Along the way the group passed through the towns of Ludlow, Aguilar, Walsenburg, Colorado City, Pueblo and finally to Fountain.

When they passed through Ludlow the local police stopped them and asked them many questions. Felix and Juan played dumb and acted like they didn't know anything about the massacre. Henry pulled out the advertisement telling the officials that they were on their way to seek employment in Fountain. After about an hour of drilling, they were dismissed.

"VAMANOS!! VAMANOS!! Let's get the hell out of here," shouted Juan. So Henry on the lead wagon directed the mules to pick up speed. Chencho had control of the second wagon and there they were in a slow gallop and followed.

"Whew, I'm sure glad that now we our on our way to the promise land, said Aurora. Those Federal agents scare me. I don't want to get shot."

"Papacito, what do we expect to find in this place called Fountain?" asked Ramona.

"Jobs, *trabajo,* opportunity and a place to raise the family and to have money and live a great life as a *familia,*" answered Felix.

Genoeva said in a whisper, "I think that I'm going to like this place called Fountain."

The travel continued through Walsenburg and then the great city of Pueblo. Pueblo was distinct, because of the big black smoke coming from the smoke stacks. About ten miles to the south of Pueblo you could see the smoke coming out of the stacks. Everyone was so intrigued by the spectacle. It was something new to all.

"So this is the city that has the great mill that makes steel, said Eduardo. Its amazing how iron can be made into this man made metal that is so strong that it actually made the Empire State building and the Brooklyn Bridge in New York City. And now all of the bridges and sky rises throughout America."

The Road to Fountain was not a paved interstate.

"How do you know so much Eduardo?" asked Chencho.

"Oh, doesn't everyone know about National Geographic," responded Eduardo.

There was a complete silence in the group, because half of the clan did not know how to read.

Many jobs were available there at the steel mill in Pueblo, but the families' destination was Fountain. This was a special place because of the personal invite to work there by Mr. Wilson. They felt welcomed and believed him that Fountain would be the place.

When they got out of the city limits of Pueblo they saw the first sign in the road that read, 30 miles to Fountain. They all started to cheer "hip hip hooray! Hip hip hooray!" Henry pulled out his harmonica and played "Adelita."

The group started to join along singing, "Adelita se llame la joven." Henry stood up on the wagon and grabbed Manuelita's hand and started to dance with her, at first she pulled away but Felix from a distance said it was okay. They all laughed and shouted *los gritos de tradicion* (traditional shouts). "Ajua! Ajua!

"Esta bien, Enrique, all is good" said Felix. Then Eduardo Duran grabbed Eloisa's hand and then they had their own baille. (Dance)

Then in an instant, Aurora shouted out, "Prisonarios! Prisonarios! Prisonarios! Mira los prisoners! Prisoners! A complete silence came to the little fiesta. The baile came to a complete halt. The families' wagons jolted to a complete stop. From a short distance you could see men working on the road with stripped suits. A police officer came up to the wagons. Everyone was somewhat apprehensive. Immediately, all of the girls and little Frankie hid under the blankets. The young men made sure that their rifles were loaded and at arms length's distance away.

"NOW SETTLE DOWN, MEJICANO!" shouted the officer. Don't worry this is the transportation maintenance crew from the state prison at Canon City, as part of their punishment they work daily on the maintenance and construction of this road from Trinidad to Colorado Springs. You have nothing to worry about; they are well guarded and will not attack, so settle down. Where are you headed?"

"We're all going to Fountain to secure some great jobs at the saw mill," said Juan.

"Well you only have about 30 more miles to travel and you are there," assured the officer. "Where are you from sir?" asked the officer.

"We're from Weston in south central Colorado. Nice place to live but now it's time to change our lives," Felix said hesitantly.

"Is that where the Ludlow tragedy happened?" asked the officer.

Felix hesitated and felt that this officer could be trusted so he continued with the whole story about being coal miners and why they left their homeland. The officer was friendly with the families and directed them to take a detour around the freshly poured concrete. The fathers were amazed about the technology that was being used to create the new road.

"Could you imagine how smooth this road will be when it's finished, replied Eduardo.

It will be in the future, automobiles will be in abundance and these old wagons will be archaic. Going to Fountain will be our future and many things will change, and who knows maybe we'll have Model A automobile, or two."

About 3 miles down the road the girls finally came out of hiding. "*No te preocupes mujeres,* don't worry ladies the coast is clear. We had those prisoners controlled from the get go. You had nothing to worry about," assured Henry. "I had my trusty trenta/trenta, Papa with his thirty odd six and hermanito with his 300 savage; we had it all under control."

Then Felix and Juan looked at each other and went into a hysterics laughing. Suddenly, Henry looked over at Manuelita and noticed that she was laughing too. He was so embarrassed that he did not talk for about 30 minutes.

The anticipation was great. From a distance one could see the big water tower that had Fountain, Colorado written on it. "We're almost there, shouted the group, just about two more miles." The wagons were weary and needed some maintenance so they rolled in slowly. The first thing they asked for was Main Street. The people in the street were all staring as if they were foreigners. Then a young boy walked up to the wagons and said, "You are on Main Street, the saw mill office is down about a block."

Slowly the group from Weston rolled down Main Street. Up ahead they were confronted by a little *Italiano*. (Italian man) Hello my name is Anthony Villani, are you here for the sawmill jobs?" asked the man.

"Yes, we've been directed by Mr. Wilson to apply for the saw mill jobs here in Fountain, replied Juan. "We have seven strong men ready to put in a day's work and make you rich. Here's the flyer." Mr. Villani took the flyer and read over it carefully. "Yep this is my flyer," certified Antonio. "That's good Mr., what shall I call you?" asked the man.

"I'm Juan Chacon, this is my lady Pimenia and these are my children; Henry, Eloisa, Delfinia and Eduardo. The other family is the Durans; Felix the father, his children Eduardo, Chencho, Manuelita, Genoeva, Jesucita, Ramona, Aurora and his two year old Francisco, who we call Frank," introduced Juan.

"So you'll need 2 cabins, one for each family," said the Villani.

"Yes Mr. Villani we'll take anything you can give us," a humbled Juan.

So Mr. Villani directed them where to go. About three miles to the west, the families found their new homes. In the same location, they found themselves amongst a colony of other families. Moving into the cabins was a hard job. The key to this move was making sure that that there was plenty of space for everyone to sleep. Could you imagine five of the Duran girls sleeping in one room? Some hours after they settled in, the colony director came in to explain the set of rules of the colony.

The families were given $20 dollars a month each in credit at the company store. Whatever excess they spent would be carried over to the next month. The children were all expected to go to school and the older young adults were required to work in the colonia and any children not going to school would also work at the mill.

The makeup of the colony was very diverse; primarily there were Mexican Americans, Italians, Slavics and Germans. All of the people were expected to assimilate, but some felt that this was an extreme goal for some wanted to keep their culture and speak their own language. Manuelita was one of those who was stubborn and refused to speak English. Henry on the other hand was open to learning everything that he could. So Henry made it a point to learn German, Italian and of course to be fluent in English.

Chapter 6

Fountain, Colorado

...Confused, fell in love, got married and raised a family.

Henry was now 20 years old and still didn't have a wife. His eye had been on Manuelita for the longest time. He recalled what his little brother had told him about a sign from La Virgen. When would I see this sign from the Blessed Virgin Mary? Daily, he would pray and asked for this miracle from God, but no sign. Manuelita was now sixteen years old. She too wondered if her future would have Henry Chacon in it.

While the men were off to work, Manuelita, Eloisa, Delfinia and Genoeva were in charge of raising the younger children and keeping the cabins clean and orderly. They were the home makers. Keeping up the chores of the homes could be very tasking. Having a career was never thought of. Their goals were based on who they'd marry. Their husbands were to be strong and hard workers. Going to college was never thought of. Pretty much being a laborer had been in their past for hundreds of years, who knows maybe since the time of the first conquistadores or the rule of the Pueblo Chieftain Pope. So the pattern of being a laborer was pretty routine. The educated and rich ruled these people. You have the money and jobs and we'll work for you. So the girls were expected to marry at a young age. After marrying they were expected to have many children. So this in itself was a great job, probably the greatest job. Raising children would keep one from wanting to set goals. One would be too busy to even think about college. Yet, who could afford it. Only rich people went to college in 1914...

After work one day, Henry stopped off at the local library in Fountain. He was looking for information on Spanish American Poetry. This was Henry's forte'. He loved to study the different forms of poetry. He was not too sure how the local people would judge him, being a Hispano who worked at the local saw mill. But being who Henry was, he never let those things bother him. The library was near closing. So Henry hurriedly walked into the library. Then in an instant there she was, one of the most beautiful women that he'd ever seen. She stood approximately 5'4"and had the most beautiful long black hair. When she faced him their eyes locked. He kept staring at her and couldn't believe how beautiful she was. He started to stutter and asked her for the poetry section of the library.

"Hello Mees, I, I, I, I'm looking for Spanish American Poetry, can you, you, you, direct me to this area," Henry said shyly and nervously.

"Si, es posible, she said in Spanish. Sure, and I speak Italian and German, also."

Then she directed him to the poetry section and conversed with him in Spanish and in English. Henry told her that he wrote his own poetry. She immediately asked him if he could share his poetry with her. He was so impressed and couldn't believe how educated this woman was. He'd never met a woman like her.

"By the way Miss, my name is Enrique Chacon, most people call me Henry," introduced the gentleman.

"Oh, by the way my name is Carmela, Carmela Caparelli" introduced Carmela.

"It's quite a pleasure Miss, I would like to share some more of my poetry with you someday," said Henry.

For the next month Henry found himself at the Library after work. Carmela was a great teacher and was so impressed with his poetry. "These poems are called alabados, poems of praise," explained Henry.

"You have some grammatical errors but I can help you with them," instructed Carmela. Henry was willing to learn anything that this beautiful woman could teach him. He was so enamored; all he could do was think about her beauty and her intelligence.

Henry walked over to the main desk at the library and asked her for a pencil. When he went over to reach for the pencil she too went for the pencil and it was like magic, their hands clasped and Henry let go quickly because he didn't know what her reaction would be. She stared at him and said, "Don't worry Enrique you are not being disrespectful." So they held each other's hand and stared into each other's eyes for minutes. Then

Henry slowly moved and their lips met. Henry was in seventh heaven and just couldn't believe how soft her lips were. He left the library slowly and when he got outside he ran home in a blaze of exhilaration. All he could do was think about those soft hands, her beautiful face, amazing smelling perfume, her inspiring words and of course those soft lips. This was the woman for him, a dream come true.

Everyone at the mill knew that Henry was a frequent visitor at the library and that he was doing more than just reciting poetry. Daily someone at the mill would pull a joke on him about Carmela, but Henry could care less. "You lumberjacks have nothing but wood for brains," retaliated Henry. Samuel the crew foreman shouted out," What are you trying to be Don Quixote? Are you following the impossible dream?"

Henry's visits to the library were quite frequent. All Henry could envision was learning and studying with Carmela. Yes he did study the poetry of Juan Cervantes and his impossible dream in the travels of Don Quixote. But in addition he studied Shakespeare, Ficini, Bacon and Petrarch. In this short time Henry had become quite the scholar. Mutually, Carmela too drew closer to Enrique's wit and intelligence.

One day after a hard day's work Henry went to the library to share more of his poetry with Carmela. He had written a special one for her. When he walked in he noticed that a different lady was sitting behind the librarian's desk. He asked for Carmela and the new librarian told him that Carmela had taken a job in Pueblo and was going back to live with her husband who she had been estranged from for two years. Henry was devastated. He couldn't believe that this lady who inspired him would do this to him. Well, Miss, do you know if she's coming back?" asked Henry.

"Don't know sir, I have no idea," replied the new Librarian.

Then Henry ran outside of the Library.

"How could she do this to me, I had such deep feelings for her and she never told me that she was married," cried Henry. Then he left the library and went behind the building and found a big rock to sit on. He sat down at put his hands over his face and wept out loud… My Carmela, my sweet Carmela, how could she do this to me," cried Henry out loud.

Then something unusual happened. As Henry left the library he walked to the local bar, to get drunk. Before he walked in he looked to the ground and saw something shiny. He grabbed the shiny object and noticed that it was a Rosary made of pure silver. The Rosary was unique because it was not complete. One of the decades of the Rosary was missing. Henry was so perplexed and believed that the Rosary was like him. His heart also had apiece torn out like the missing decade on the silver Rosary.

"Could this be the sign that I've been waiting for. Are you talking to me Lord? Are you giving me a sign my Virgen? Do you want me to marry Manuelita?" Cried Henry... So instead of going into the bar Henry found himself walking home and praying the Rosary.

Back at the Duran cabin something strange was in the works. Manuelita had just gone to bed and had fallen into a deep sleep. She found herself walking in the sierra, what seemed to be the forest near her home in Weston. Walking in the woods was one of her favorite pastimes. In her journey through the forest she'd found a little wooden box. Where ever she went in the forest someone was trying to take this box from her. In the distance she heard a faint distant voice calling out to her. Manuelita, Manuelita, I need you, I want you. Manuelita walked toward the voice and when she got to its location no one was there. Then in the back ground she heard a voice that sounded similar to Henry's and he said, "look into the box, you will find out your future." Manuelita was so frightened that she ran as fast as she could toward home. She then became totally confused... Where am I going, I'm lost thought Manuelita. "I can't find my way, please God help me!" she prayed out loud. Then she heard a loud voice, WAKE UP! WAKE UP! MAUELITA WAKE UP. Then Chencho was over looking her in her bed and said, "wake up your having a nightmare."

Manuelita then woke up trembling. Chencho was very comforting to her. No te preocupes mi hermanita, don't worry my little sister all is fine. You were having a bad sueno (dream.). "Oh did you forget something last night," asked Chencho?

"What do you mean, my brother," asked Manuelita?

"Oh someone brought this by last evening and said it belonged to Manuelita, said Chencho.

"What is it," asked Manuelita?

"I don't know, but it looks like a wooden box," said Chencho.

"A box, a box, a little wooden box!" said Manuelita in amazement.

She was so surprised, because it looked like the box in her dream. She had remembered that in her dream a voice had said that her future was in this box. Now could this be reality?

"Open it! Open it!" Chencho said anxiously.

Manuelita trembled as she tried to open the box and said, "I can't, I can't, you open it Chencho."

Then all of the sisters came into the room and said, "What's going on?"

Chencho opened the little box and said, "Look it's a decade of the Rosary and it's made of pure silver. Pura plata, it will be worth some money."

Then Manuelita shared the dream with her siblings. Manuelita looked up to the heavens and said, "My future is in this box. And asked, what am I suppose to be a nun or something?"

Then Genoeva said, "Maybe this is a sign from La Virgen." Now I'm more confused than ever.

"What am I supposed to do now, prepare for the convent," said Manuelita.

Manuelita didn't put two and two together and forgot that the voice in the dream had come from Henry, well it sounded like Henry. So the story continues. In one month the local priest was to be into town to make his monthly visit. Manuelita's plan was to visit the priest and share her dream with him and see if her destiny would be a nun. Manuelita had made many visits to the church and would go to the Blessed Sacrament to ask that question, if she was going to be a Nun. Her prayers were unceasing. Daily novenas, rosaries, and fasting became part of her daily routine.

Big brother Eduardo Duran wanted to sell the silver rosary. He felt that the extra money would help out with the expenses of the household. Juan said that the rosary was a gift from God and that it was supposed to be part of the family's heirloom. It really did mean that to Manuelita, for it was her treasure and no was going to take it from her.

Next door, in the top drawer of Henry's dresser lies the rest of the rosary. Henry still healing from the pain of a broken heart had almost forgotten about the rosary. All he could do was think about his lost love. So he wrote a poem to send to her in Pueblo.

Carmela

Carmela, Carmela, where are you today?
I miss you so much,
Why did you go astray?
You will be in my dreams always
I needed you to stay.
Next to my heart remember that day,
When we laughed and sang about that possible day.

We'd finally be together in May...
Oh Carmela, Carmela,
Why did you break my heart and go away?

Henry was unsuccessful in his quest of Carmela's address. He asked everyone who knew her, but to no avail. He was so distraught that he would visit the bar to have a couple of drinks with the other lumber jacks. He made sure that he went home late, so that his father and Pimenia wouldn't hear him come in. Juan was too smart for his son. He knew that his son had been visiting the librarian and that he was falling in love with the young Italiana. So he gave him a lot of time to mourn the loss of his love.

The next morning Eloisa asked Henry if he'd heard the news about Manuelita.

"Buenos dias, Enrique. Have you heard the news about Manuelita," asked Eloisa?

"What's that?" asked Henry.

"Some people believe that La Virgen has given her a sign to become a nun, a sister, like Mother Cabrini, explained Eloisa. She found a rosary made of pure plata, well, at least part of one part of a one."

"What do you mean part of one?" asked Henry.

Its only one decade, an Our Father and ten Hail Marys, one decade, eleven pure silver beads, explained Eloisa. She truly believes that being a sister in the future is a great possiblity.

"Where did she find this part of a rosary?" asked Henry.

"It was delivered to her cabin and no can remember who delivered it, said Eloisa. It was in a little wooden box and the night before, she had a dream that a voice told her, that what was inside the box, was in her future. She said that there was a voice in the dream that sounded similar to yours Henry, Henry, yours. Some believe that an angel brought this little wooden box to her." Do you believe that it's a message from La Virgen?"

Henry sat there in a stare and pondered the moment. Eloisa sat there waiting for Henry to give her a definitive answer.

"Henry, are you okay?" asked Eloisa.

"Yes, yes I'm okay, todo esta bien, everything is okay, answered Henry. I don't believe that it's a message from La Virgen, but just coincidental."

"Well Henry you can believe what you want, but Manuelita is very serious about this little wooden box and the silver decade of the Rosary," said Eloisa.

Henry went off to work. The guys at the mill found out about the rosary. There was so much discussion about the rosary; the mill boss had to get on the crew for slowing down production. Henry just laughed to himself and thought the incident was funny. Eduardo and Chencho were getting tired of all the questions that were getting asked.

Later during lunch break Henry and his brother Eduardo were talking about the Rosary ordeal. Henry was reminded by Eduardo about the discussion they had when they first met Manuelita.

"Henry do you recall the discussion we had when you first met Manuelita?" asked Eduardo.

"Yes sort of," said Henry.

"It looks like Manuelita got her message, did you?" asked Eduardo.

"What do you mean little brother?" asked Henry.

"Did La Virgen give you a message?" asked Eduardo.

"Little hermanito, tonight when we get home I'll show you something that is very interesting and might be the answer to Manuelita's future," said Henry.

"Oh Eduardo, Eduardo what makes you so fat, a piece of corn bread and a tail of a rat," Ohhhh, Eduardo, Eduardo what makes you so fat, a piece of corn and a tail of a rat," sang Henry.

Henry tried to get his mind off Carmela so periodically he'd sing a song or two. This seemed to help Henry's broken heart.

Later that night at the Chacon's supper table the discussion was about the little wooden box that was delivered to Manuelita's cabin. Juan was very bewildered by the situation. He was a very faithful servant to the Blessed Virgen. He asked the opinion of his children. Henry played dumb and acted like he didn't know anything about the little wooden box. Eduardo seemed somewhat naïve and didn't share too much of an opinion. Delfinia was a true believer and helped Manuelita find information about the religious life of a sister. Eloisa was not quite sure but wanted to be supportive.

"Well whatever happens to Manuelita we need to support her a hundred per cent," encouraged Juan. "Next week Father Antonio Garcia from Colorado Springs will be here to celebrate mass with us. Manuelita is going to meet with him and get some spiritual direction.

It will be quite an honor to know that there is a possibility that she will be a religious and she's sort of, like part of the familia." Then Juan's eyes filled with tears. God only knows the outcome of this. If she's meant to be a nun it will be great, but if not, it will be God's Will. So as a family let's go into the bedroom and pray a rosary to ask La Virgen through Jesus Cristo for guidance."

In the homes of many of the people was a family altar. The Juan Chacon familia made it a habit to pray the Rosary. They would go into the room that had that special altar made. At the center of most altars was a crucifix. Then the family would have a family Bible. In many altars there were pictures of saints and the heavenly Cherubim. In the case of Juan Chacon's altar were his ancestors' pictures or portraits.

After the rosary was recited that night, Henry secretly showed his silver rosary with four decades and one; yes one decade missing to Eduardo. He knew that it was not time to share his secret with the entire family. "Eduardo, little hombre I want to show you something, said Henry. This is the rosary that I found near the library. It's made of pure silver, pura plata."

"You've got to be kidding big brother, Wow, its pure silver. Que bonito, how beautiful! It's a sure sign that Manuelita's your future woman…"said Eduardo excitedly.

"Now let's take this a little *mas despacio,* a little slower, said Henry. I don't want you to jump to any conclusions."

"Big brother this is the sign that you've been looking for since Weston, when you first saw Manuelita. How are you going to tell Manuelita about the other piece?" asked Ed. You are going to have to handle this very delicately. Boy this is the most excitement I've ever experienced in my life."

"Now little brother, don't tell anyone, not anyone until Manuelita meets with Father Antonio, replied Henry. It will take a lot of time to figure this one out. I can trust you. So remember no one."

Come Sunday morning the Duran family prepared for the big meeting with Father Antonio. Manuelita got up extra early and made sure that everything would be perfect. With the help of Genoeva, Manuelita looked extra beautiful. Genoeva made sure that her big sister would be the most beautiful woman in Fountain. There she stood, four foot nine about a hundred pounds and

Simultaneously, the Durans and Chacons walked out the front doors of their cabins. Henry looked over to the Duran cabin and couldn't believe how beautiful Manuelita looked that morning. She looked like a goddess. He just kept staring or should I say more like gawking at her with mouth wide open. Good thing that there weren't any flies because for breakfast he'd have an extra mouthful.

By wagon the Durans and Chacons traveled to Holy family Church in Fountain. On the trip, Henry couldn't keep his eyes off of Manuelita. Eduardo Duran yelled out, "quit staring at my little sister and put your eye balls back in your eye sockets, before I…"

Juan looked at his son and told him, "*mas respecto mi hijito*, show more respect my son."

But Henry was having a very hard time with this moment. He thought to himself, she looks like a little beautiful little angel. I've never seen anyone as beautiful. She's prettier than Carmela. Could this become reality, Manuelita and Henry? I can't believe what you are telling me Lord.

When they arrived at the church there were people waiting to see Manuelita and her silver rosario. They had just gotten there in time for the Mass so there wasn't any time for visiting. Father Antonio was quite the homilist. His theme for the Mass was about miracles in the history of the church. The emphasis was "blessed are those who believe without seeing" and that God performs miracles every day. As preached that day…

"Brothers and sisters of Holy Family Parish, I come to you in total humility and love. Now is the time to believe in our Lord Jesus Christ. He comes to each of us daily to comfort us in our times of struggle, grief, despair and joy. Now brothers and sisters, there have been many people in this community who have been talking about a silver rosary with several decades missing. That this one decade was delivered in a little wooden box and that it's possible that an angel delivered it! Now we know that in scripture, in II Corinthians 5:7 of the Bible, that Jesus, yes Jesus said, "Blessed are those who believe without seeing." Now is the time to have faith! Is it time to be blinded by Faith to see? Do you believe without seeing? Is your faith strong even in good and bad times? Jesus said that even you will do greater things than I. Jesus loves you so much that He gives you this gift…It is evident through all of the tragedies through losing a child at birth to tragic deaths on the dangerous jobs that you do you still find ways to come back on your knees to Jesus Christ…That is Faith! Now about this little wooden box, some believe that it was delivered by an angel, of course it was. Jesus delivers little wooden boxes to us every day of our lives. It is our responsibility to accept these boxes as gifts directly from God. Now, if I was a Baptist Minister, at this time I would be asking for an amen. Have you received your box like Manuelita? Have you accepted your box? When we accept the little gifts from God in our lives, it's called Grace. Many times He gives us gifts and we don't accept them and then we cry out, why me Lord, why me Lord? Now go out and celebrate Jesus to His fullest and say yes to Him daily. Amen…"

After Mass, Manuelita went back to the sacristy to talk with Father Antonio. The people of the community waited patiently outside to hear the outcome of the meeting. Father asked Manuelita to review everything about her dream. Then Father emphasized in the important parts of the homily that he'd given earlier at Mass. He recommended that Jesus has given her a special gift and that she needed to follow her heart. He believed that the rest of the rosary would be revealed to her in the future and that she needed to be patient.

"Manuelita, I assure you that in due time God will reveal the message of the silver decade in the wooden box," said Father Antonio. "Follow what your heart is telling you and it will be God's grace that will lead you in the right path. I cannot tell you to become a nun, who knows in the future, you might be a special mother with many children and great grandchildren. The important thing is to believe, have faith and accept God's gifts daily."

Manuelita was very bewildered by the priest's suggestion. She exited the sacristy and went outside where the congregation was waiting. She looked up to the crowd and said, "I must be patient and follow my heart. God will reveal to me in the future the truth. There is a great possibility that I could be a nun or a mother with many children and grandchildren. So be patient with me and remember the Father's homily, to believe without seeing."

Many of the people were disappointed with the answer and didn't like what she had said; I guess they all wanted to see a miracle. People began to call out and shout this was a sham.

Felix was a smart man he got everyone into the wagon quickly and they all sped off to their homes. Felix made sure that Manuelita was safe from the enraged crowd. Manuelita was a strong young woman and was confused, yet pleased with the Father's suggestion. She ignored the insults but all who knew the Durans were very supportive of Manuelita.

Days had passed slowly and still no message. Manuelita became very anxious to follow her heart. She thought where is my heart taking me to? I need another sign from La Virgen to find out where I will be in the future.

"Senora La Virgen, I need you to console me and have a discussion with the Heavenly hosts, I need to know soon," prayed Manuelita. Daily, she'd pray her rosary and asked for divine intervention to help answer her question.

Next door at the cabin of the Chacons lies Henry in his bed. In deep contemplation he went over in his mind, what he needed to do to make it right with Manuelita. In the bed next to his, lies Eduardo. "Little brother what should I do? I need to make this right with Manuelita. What should I do?" questioned Henry.

"Don't worry, the plan is simple, we need to find a way to get the two pieces of the rosary together," said Eduardo.

"What do you mean?" asked Henry, as he twirled the partial rosary in his hand.

"The only thing is, you will probably have to marry her, said Ed. It's probably the smart thing to do. I believe that you are ready to marry this good woman. I truly believe that you too have received the message of La Virgen, my big brother. Henry, she is your gift, will you accept it?" asked Ed.

Henry sat quietly for about twenty minutes and finally responded, "I do want this woman to be Manuelita Chacon and I want her to be the mother of my children."

"That's what I want to hear brother, but now what do we do to make this miracle happen?" asked Eduardo.

"Let's sleep on it and look at all of our options and ask for divine intervention," replied Henry.

So that night, Henry went into a deep sleep. He found himself at the mill where he was unloading lumber. His job was to unload a wagon loaded with pine logs. The peculiar thing was that every time that he'd unload a log, a log was added.

The mill boss came around and said, "Henry, you haven't even put a dent in that load! What are you doing?"

Henry tried to plead his case, but no one would believe him.

"Come on *huevon* (lazy), you are slowing down production," yelled out the boss.

"I'm trying my hardest, but a log is added every time I take one out!" pleaded Henry.

Henry was then replaced by Chencho and one log at a time Chencho had the wagon unloaded.

"See Henry, it takes a real man to unload a wagon made out of that kind of wood. Can't you see that? It also takes a real man to give Manuelita the rest of her rosary... Do think that the Lord is not watching you?" reminded Chencho.

"The mill boss then moved Henry to a different wagon to unload.

"Henry we need to step up production so give it your best," directed the boss. We don't need you to slow us down, so work harder!"

Then the routine would start all over again, Henry would pull a log off the wagon and then one was added, one was pulled and then one was added. Henry couldn't believe his eyes, he then grumbled to himself.

"I WILL NEVER BE ABLE TO FINISH THIS JOB," yelled out Henry! SOMEONE HELP ME! SOMEONE! PLEASE SOMEONE!"

Then Eduardo and Felix Duran came over to the wagon full of logs and found Henry in a very precarious position. He was a total mess. Sweat was dripping down his face and his hair. He also had blood dripping from his hands from the extra hard work from pulling thousands of logs from the wagons. No one acknowledged the hard work that he'd done, but only thought of him as being lazy...

"Henry, Manuelita wants her rosary, her rosary, her rosary, her rosary, her silver rosary, her rosary Henry, her rosary Henry..."

"HELP ME, HELP ME, HELP ME, HELP ME, PLEASE LORD HELP ME!" cried out Henry.

"Wake up Henry, wake up, wake up my son, you were having *una pesadilla;* a night mare... said Juan. Don't worry my son everything is okay..."

"I can't unload any more logs, no more logs, please no more!" cried out, Henry.

"Son you are at home safe in your bed, not at work. Calmate my son, your safe here with us Calmate!" said Juan, as he tried to comfort his son.

"But she wants her rosary, her rosary," cried Henry.

"It's just a dream, *una pesadilla, mi niño,* just a nightmare my son" comforted Juan.

When he was wide awake he realized that it was only a dream and was thankful that it wasn't reality. It was a *sueno,* a dream with a message.

Here is a cup of tea you have about two more hours before it's time to go to work. I'll make you some breakfast before you go to work, said Eloisa.

"Thanks, little sister," said Henry graciously.

The rest of the Chacon abode was in awe when they realized that Henry's dream was about a rosary.

"A rosary, a rosary why was he shouting out, she wants her rosary, said little Delfinia. The only discussion about a rosary comes from Manuelita's rosary next door."

That morning Henry went off to work and was tentative about unloading logs. He was extra quiet that day and every wagon that he unloaded was unloaded quickly. Henry found himself throughout the day thinking about the dream. What was the dream telling me? Eduardo his brother met with him during the lunch break and assured him that that dream was so real that he heard its message. "It's time big brother, its time," said Eduardo.

Traditionally the people of this era had a different belief when it came to courtship due to the economic situation and religious belief. The tradition was that there was no courtship. The families were very poor. The idea of going out to a movie or a date was not even an option. There were only movie houses in the big cities. Parents would not allow their daughters to date for fear of pregnancy. It was taboo to be pregnant out of wedlock. It was against societal norms and the regulations of Roman Catholic Church. If you were interested in someone you'd write a letter asking for the young lady's hand in marriage. Usually the young man would write this letter and then the letter would be delivered by other members of the family to the lady's parents. If the young lady was interested she would discuss all possibilities with her parents. If the proposal was accepted a letter would be returned in ten days saying that the engagement was in preparation. If the proposal was not accepted, a pumpkin (*Calabasa*) would be returned to the person who proposed by the other family members saying, "Thanks but no thanks."

Manuelita was close to her seventeenth birthday when she found the rosary's silver decade and Henry was close to twenty one. In comparison to other's married at this time their ages were in the acceptable range of marriage. The extended family was the tradition of the family which included the grandparents the children and the grandchildren. The living quarters were usually a two room house which would make it very inconvenient for everyone. When one is use to these arrangements, one does not know anything else.

It was the big moment for the Chacon clan. Henry presented his part of the rosary to his family. "It's time for me, familia to settle down, find a wife and have me some little Henrys," joked Henry.

"What are you talking about my son?" asked Juan.

"This is what I'm talking about," said Henry.

He then pulled out the other part of the silver Rosary. The rest of the family went ecstatic. They couldn't believe their eyes. Taking turns holding it and admiring it, they were sure that this was a true gift from God.

"Que bonito es, how beautiful it is, said Delfinia. I can't believe my eyes. It's a true miracle."

"Well are you going to ask Manuelita to marry you?" asked Eloisa.

"That's the plan, but I wanted to share this secret that I've been holding so dear to my heart for the longest time, said Henry. We'll have to write the letter and one or two of you will have to make the delivery. If she says yes, she'll write an acceptance letter and if the answer is no, she'll send a pumpkin…I sure hope that it's not the calavasa."

"Now who's going to help me write this letter?" asked Henry, as he gestured with his hands folded.

The letter was a team effort; everyone added their two cents to the letter.

Delfinia said, "Tell her that you love her."

Eduardo added, "Write something about that this would be a marriage made in heaven."

"My son, formally, tell compadre Felix that you will support her and treat her like a queen, fathers like that kind of language, it's assurance that their daughter will be protected," said Juan.

Eloisa added, "You need to include something about how much you will treat her with respect and don't forget to insert the other part of the Rosary in the envelope. By doing this they will know that it is a gift from heaven. Could you imagine the expression that will be on her face, when she sees the other part of the rosary?"

"Now, who is going to deliver this letter?" asked Henry, as he paced back and forth in the front room of the cabin.

"Oh before you ask her to marry you; you'll need to ask Antonio Villani if he has another cabin available for you and Manuelita, said Juan and you'll need to set up arrangements with Father Antonio who lives in Colorado Springs. So time is of the essence."

The next day Henry and Juan met with Antonio Villani. They discussed their plans with him. Antonio thought that he could set up a cabin for Henry and Manuelita; Henry told Antonio that these were his plans and she hadn't accepted yet. She hadn't received the letter of proposal yet either. Antonio thought that Henry was an asset to the mill so he gave Henry two weeks to set up his plan.

That evening Juan and Eloisa volunteered to deliver the letter next door. Juan and Eloisa dressed for the occasion. They walked over to the cabin next door and knocked until someone answered.

"Enter, enter my friends, Felix said cordially. What can I do for you my great friends?"

"Compadre, Eloisa and I come to you with a proposal," said Juan. "I'll leave this letter with you and family to discuss what you might want to do. Thank you, and if her answer is yes in ten days she'll write a letter with an approval and if the answer is no, send us a pumpkin. Thank you and have a good night."

"Bueno compadre, you'll get your answer in ten days, soon, not to delay any plans that you may have," said Felix.

Little did Juan know that since Manuelita's meeting with Father Antonio, Manuelita had received three letters of proposal from other gentlemen. She had no interest in the other guys, so they received big orange pumpkins delivered by Eduardo and Chencho Duran.

"Manuelita here is another proposal, said Felix. You'll be surprised at who wants your hand in marriage."

Manuelita came out of the bedroom where she had been praying the rosary. Who was here Papa?" asked Manuelita.

"It was my compadre Juan and his daughter Eloisa, said Felix. Enrique Henry Chacon has written you a letter of proposal."

"Who, Henry Chacon, asked Manuelita? Manuelita couldn't believe her eyes. The first thing she saw was the other part of the rosary in the letter's envelope. Instantaneously tears came profusely down her cheeks. It had to be a *milagro* (miracle) from God. "So it was Henry's voice that I heard in the dream," she cried loudly. The other members of the family gathered around her and couldn't believe their eyes. Felix was touched by the experience, he too cried and then all of the other members of the family joined in and all hugged each other and knew that Manuelita's future would be close to home with Henry Chacon.

The night was a very long one for Manuelita. She couldn't sleep. Over and over in her head she could hear her mother telling her to watch out for that Henry Chacon, all he likes to do is socialize and chase women. But what was the message God was telling her through the rosary? Who do I trust? The priest said, "Follow your heart." Tossing and turning Manuelita couldn't fall asleep and made the night miserable for the other sisters who were also sleeping in her bed. Follow your heart, a message from heaven was repeated in her head.

The next day Eduardo and Chencho Duran had a scheme. The two conjured up a plan to fool Henry about his proposal. On the ninth day of the ten days of waiting they would sneak over to the Chacon cabin and deliver a big orange pumpkin. Felix didn't know anything about this, but if he did the two would have been in dire straits.

"Chencho *ven pa ca*, come here, I have a plan that I want to pull on ole Enrique. He's so in love with our sister, we have to keep reminding him that she is our sister and that we are not going to let her go that easily," whispered Eduardo Duran.

"I don't know if that's a very nice thing to do," whispered Chencho.

"Oh come on, it'll be a lot of fun and no one will ever find out,' challenged Eduardo Duran.

So the two boys stayed up late that night and told their father that they needed to get more firewood for the cold night. The two went around the back of the cabin where Eduardo stored a big orange pumpkin for this special occasion. When they got to the cabin the Chacon's dogs, Lelo and Pokey started to bark. In an instant, the Chacon's lantern lights went on.

"Hurry up, Eduardo said, "I don't want them to see us."

When the Duran boys got home they couldn't stop laughing.

Felix yelled out, "Callete, Callete, be quiet, quiet, your sisters are trying to sleep!

When the Chacons received the message of the pumpkins they couldn't believe that this had happen. Henry again, went through the pain of losing another woman that he loved immensely.

"How could she do this to me, asked Henry? Why me Lord? Why me? She and I are a marriage meant in heaven. This is impossible everything was perfect until this big orange pumpkin ended up on our front porch." It couldn't be more perfect," cried out Henry.

"Calm down my son there has to be an explanation," said Juan. The pumpkin came a day early and compadre Felix knows the tradition of the pumpkin very well, I don't think that he'd break the tradition by sending the pumpkin on the ninth day. I believe that there is horse play here. I'll go have a talk with him," said Juan.

On the tenth day Manuelita and her family met after supper to discuss the proposal of Henry Chacon. "Now we have very a big decision to make here, said Felix. My daughter, I know that you will make a great wife. Do you believe that Henry will make great husband? Now set aside the miracle of the Rosary, do you believe that he will support you till the end and be a great father? Now I know at the mill that Henry is a good hard worker. Now, set aside his jokes and poetry, which could be very entertaining and irritating, will you be happy with this man named Enrique Chacon?"

Manuelita was very quiet and then she slowly pulled out the silver

Rosary and said, "This is all I need, the message is muy claro, the message is clear. Yes papa, yes papa, I want this man to be my husband till I die."

For a moment there was complete silence in the cabin and then with complete exhilaration the girls all shouted, "Manuelita's going to get married!"

"Okay boys now it's time to deliver the letter next door but this time I'm going with you," demanded Felix.

On the way to the Chacon cabin, Felix and the boys ran into Juan as he was walking to their cabin. Felix handed over the letter of approval and Juan accepted it. Juan said, "that's funny last night we received a big orange pumpkin and we thought that that the answer was no."

"Oh no compadre, I told you that you'd get your answer on the tenth day and here is the letter. Congratulations Juan, we're going to be familia!" shouted Felix.

Next door Henry waited patiently at the entrance of the porch. Juan handed over the letter to Henry; he read it and shouted for joy. He knew that it was a marriage made in heaven. Eloisa and Delfinia were so happy that they couldn't sleep all night. They talked about the wedding and the great celebration that would take place. Eduardo was so happy and reminded Henry about the great sign of La Virgen.

On November 17, 1914 my Grandparents Maria Manuelita Duran and Jose Enrique Henry Chacon became husband and wife. They were married by Father Antonio Garcia in Colorado Springs, Colorado. The mode of transportation to Colorado Springs was a borrowed horse and buggy. The rest of the families followed in wagons pulled by mules. They didn't have a wedding ring to signify their marriage, but a rosary, a very special silver rosary. A rosary was a common symbol that represented the vows in those days. Today, the common symbol is a ring. This sacred marriage marked the beginning of the next generation that will have a great imprint on many more lives to come.

Chapter 7

The New Generation

...Great expectations and Hope bring life...

The early morning came on that Monday November 19th, 1914. As Henry opened the bedroom window he could smell the fresh air, and it couldn't smell any fresher. Manuelita and Henry were on their honeymoon in their newly acquired cabin. It seemed sort of strange for Manuelita to share her bed with her husband instead of her four sisters. Manuelita knew the routine, get up early, make the coffee and breakfast and Henry would then be off to work. Except for today Henry was given one day off from work to celebrate his honey moon with his new bride.

It didn't take too long for Henry and Manuelita to conceive. In a matter of two months she was with child. The news swept the Chacons and Durans, the coming child would be a paramount moment for both families. On December 14th, 1915, Manuelita gave birth to Maria de la Luz Chacon later known as Lucy. The families were ecstatic and so thrilled to have someone to love in common. She was so cute and chubby. Maria de la Luz was her baptismal name. Traditionally the majority of Catholic females would take on the name Maria and the males would take the name Jose. But there was some exceptions to the rule, their might be a Jesus or a Juan. It was a tradition, how could one go wrong with a name like Maria and Jose, the names of the parents of Jesus... As Henry best put it, "with joy and happiness God is always by our side... He brought the light, Maria de la Luz Chacon into our lives..." The progeny continued, when the Chacons brought their second child into this world. His name was Eugenio; he would be the one to carry the name onto the next generations, born July 13th 1917. On that momentous day Henry and Manuelita declared Eugenio a genius, having great hope that this little one would one day take them out of poverty. Then the following came on June 24th 1920 with Juan Bautista Chacon, Henry Christened him a musician and entertainer…

Chapter 8

1920
Moonshine or Influenza

...In the World not of the World...
John 17:14

The year was 1920. World War I had just ended and "The Roaring 20's" had just begun. To the south in Mexico, Francisco Pancho Villa was running havoc with the second Mexican Revolution. Back East the Methodists, Northern Baptists, Southern Baptists, Presbyterians, Disciples, Congregationalists, Quakers, and Scandinavian Lutherans with their temperance agenda pulled off a strong campaign to outlaw the manufacture, transportation, import, export, and sale of alcoholic beverages. At any time, possession of liquor, wine or beer was illegal. On January 16th, 1920 the 18th Amendment was ratified by the majority vote of all the states. This meant that all places of alcoholic consumption would be disbanded throughout the United States. It wasn't until 1933; the 18th amendment was repealed with 21st amendment.

The reaction of this new law was met with different sentiment. But the owners of the places of serving the alcoholic beverages were the most resistant. Thus illegal alcoholic production was prevalent throughout the United States and Fountain was no exception... The Black market was a huge business during prohibition.

"Henry, what do you think about the new prohibition law?" asked Chencho.

"Don't really have too much of an opinion, all I know is that, that Lou at the Fountain Saloon is pretty mad now that he has to close his joint," replied Chencho.

"That's too bad; doesn't the government realize the loss the common business saloon owner is going to suffer?" I believe that there will be all sorts of illegal alcohol production and criminal activity throughout the U.S." commented Henry.

"It's going to be one major problema," said Chencho.

"The United States has voted, and now we must abide by its laws, said Chencho. The Methodists and other pious Christian religions back east have convinced the rest of the America that alcohol is evil and that it's the main cause for many ills of our society. The rest of the states must be in agreement because now we are subjected by this law. You can drink alcohol in your own privacy but it cannot be sold in a place of business."

"I like to have a *trago* (drink) now and then, I hope I don't get into trouble," said Henry.

The young men went off to work at the mill. The conversation at the mill was about the new law of prohibition. Some were in favor and some were vehemently against the law. Many of the men felt that now a lot of hooch (illegal whiskey) was going to be produced, distributed and consumed illegally.

Back at the Henry and Manuelita residence, the children were all living a healthy and joyous life. Lucy was five, Eugenio three and Juan one. Manuelita still at a young age of 22 and Henry at 26 were very happy raising their children. Grandpa Felix, Chencho and the rest of the Durans moved in with them. Eloisa, Henry's sister would marry Juan Griego and Delfinia, Eduardo and Grandpa Juan and Pimenia would move in with them. Times were getting somewhat rough at the mill so Tony Villani had to combine some of the cabins to make his business profitable. Eduardo Duran was married two years earlier to Margarita and moved out and sought a business on his own as a carpenter. Genoeva was in love with Julian Martinez a railroad worker. The time was near and Genoeva too would leave the Duran abode.

At the Juan Chacon cabin, Eloisa and her new husband Juan Isidro Griego took in a distant cousin of Juan's. His name was Tomas Sanchez. He came from Alamosa in the San Luis Valley. He was also hired to work at the mill. His experience was very vital. He'd been working in a forest near Capulin. He was a well respected man, so it seemed, the only thing or vice that he had was a strong love for his home made whisky. Tomas was also an honored soldier in World War I with a purple heart to show that that he was wounded in battle. His most apparent feature was his gimp; this is where he took grenade shrapnel to the back of his right leg.

"Primo, it's really nice to be back home. Now all I have to do is find me a nice senorita like you, Juan Isidro," said Tomas.

Eloisa turned red with embarrassment. "She is some good lookin' woman, I guess, I just have the charm and looks," joked Juan. "Some refer to me as Don Juan, the real "Latin lover."

Then everyone in the cabin roared with laughter.

"You know tomorrow is going to be my first day at the mill. Mr. Villani was very gracious by letting me have a job," said Tomas. "I will not let him down. I sure hope that I will not be an inconvenience to you all."

"No es problema, we'll all need to support one another while Tomas is here with us. En un rato (short time) Juan and Eloisa have their own cabin to start their own familia," said Juan.

"Tell us about Europe, Tomas. I always wanted to go abroad and defend our country," said Eduardo Chacon.

"Well my friend, Europe is made up of many countries. The majority of the fighting took place in Germany. That's where I was wounded," explained Tomas.

At this time Tomas pulled up his right pant leg. Half of his calf muscle was missing. They all couldn't believe their eyes. It seemed as if, with that little bit of muscle he wouldn't be able to walk, but he was a very strong man and was able to get around despite his limp.

After seeing this Eduardo had second thoughts about war. "Tomas we are so proud of you for defending our nation," said Delfinia. You only read about such feats, and now we have an actual person in front of us who has experienced it, what an honor!"

"Okay, we all have to get up early and be refreshed for a hard day's work at the mill, said Juan.

Buenas noches." (Good night)

The next day Tomas met Henry and the rest of the Durans. Chencho and Tomas hit it off immediately. It seemed as if they knew each other forever. The rest of the crew accepted Tomas and his skill in cutting the long pines.

"Say Chencho, what do you do here for entertainment?" asked Tomas.

"I never really think about it too much, all we do is work, work, work," said Chencho.

"What do you all do on weekends when there is no work?" asked Tomas.

"We rest, just rest. Go to church on Sundays, if the priest comes from Colorado Springs. Besides that, we just rest. Can't drink cause it's illegal and don't have a woman yet. I do have my eye on a couple, but not yet," said Chencho.

"What about Eduardo Chacon, what's he up to? He's just a kid almost 20 years old and many young ladies are attracted to him. Does he like the moonshine?" asked Tomas.

"What's moonshine?" asked Chencho.

"Whisky, hooch, illegal drink," answered Tomas.

"What do you know about it?" asked Chencho.

"We made it in Germany, my buddy and I made it and served the rest of our platoon. Canadian Whiskey goes down smooth as silk. When it comes to making whiskey we are experts. My buddy was originally from Canada and then became a citizen of the United States. I'm expecting him to move to Fountain. He is an expert in brewing Canadian style whiskey."

"You can't bring that into our family that will destroy our great standing here in Fountain!" exclaimed Chencho.

For about a month there was never a conversation about the moonshine, until one day a stranger came into the town. His name was Bill Berkman. He was that friend that Tomas Sanchez had been waiting for, Tomas' friend from World War I and business partner.

Bill was one of those people who had some fortune, inheritance made him somewhat comfortable in his financial status. Outside of Fountain, Bill bought forty five acres in the wooded area west near Carson. He built his own cabin and pretty much was isolated in a remote area where no one would bother him. Eventually, Tomas moved out of Juan Chacon's cabin and moved in with him. Now by this time many of the workers had their own Model T's. With no exception so did Bill.

In time, Bill found himself working at the mill, but was this a cover up? Tomas and Bill made themselves available to the workers at the mill, but in which way?

"You know Tomas it sure is nice to be back in business. It will be a matter of weeks and we'll have full production and we'll be the richest men this side of the Mississippi, retorted Bill.

This distiller should work at its maxim as soon as we get all of the pipes, pots and filters from the hardware store. This can't be a hillbilly operation.

People need not know where our still is. We take the merchandise outside the factory and make our sale in definite secret places and can only trust a few. Just like in Germany we'll make the best Canadian whisky in Colorado. How ironic this can be, Canadian whisky in Germany and now Canadian whisky in Colorado."

"Either we'll be the richest or we'll be spending time in the penitentiary breaking our backs doing hard time. This has to be a smooth operation," stated Tomas as he grabbed a pick and hit the ground.

"Do you think we can trust those Chacon and Duran brothers? Who would suspect them, they go to church and are well respected at the mill and town, who would trust them? Probably everyone," asked Bill as he unloaded ears of corn from his new Model T truck."

"No, a big no, they are family and I don't want to involve them," shouted Tomas as he slammed the front screen door. "

"What about Juan Isidro, the big guy, I bet he could probably whoop some ass if we got into a scuffle," said Bill.

"No! Not even him. I guarantee you that in a few weeks there will be some young men that we can trust and incorporate into our business," assured Tomas.

The two bootleggers continued to empty out the truck. They planned and talked all night about their illegal business. The next morning they drove to the mill and continued to fit in with the rest of the crew. During the week everyone talked about the barn dance that was going to take place at the Dubois farm east of Fountain. A local band was going to play traditional Mexican, Country and Western music. The entire community was invited and of course Henry Chacon would be the square dance caller.

After work Tomas and Bill met and on the way home they made a plan to try to sell some of their moonshine. This would be a great opportunity to make their first sales. The plan was to give some of the men at the dance free samples to hook them on the taste of the Canadian style whisky. They felt that if they gave the samples to the younger men it would probably be the best way to spread the news about this vintage whisky.

The dance started at nine pm and everyone was there, all the families, even children. Whenever there was a dance in the community everyone would come. The composition was pretty diverse, people from all cultural backgrounds. There were Mexican Americans; some called themselves Spanish Americans because of the dispute down south in Mexico, Italians, Slavics and many who'd been here for generations just called themselves

Americans. Many of the Americans were a mixture of many ethnic backgrounds and lost track of their identity as the generations passed. But the person who would bring the group together was Henry Chacon. The dance started sharply at nine pm., with a waltz. One two three, one two three, the men would chose a partner. There was some discrimination where the Spanish and Mexican American people would dance the waltzes together and the other ethnic groups would select their own.

Young Eduardo Chacon now a young twenty year old, was prime to go out and find himself a young senorita. The girls were enamored by Eduardo and his fine looks. It seemed as if every young girl in town knew who he was. Eduardo loved to dance, so he would ask all the Spanish and Mexican American girls to dance. The other girls too would want to dance with Eduardo, but it was taboo to interact with the other cultures in public settings. It really didn't matter too much to Eduardo because he was having too much fun with all the girls.

The square dance was a different story. It was like a big game where all the ethnic groups would get involved. It was a common way of erasing all racism and bigotry. The most important thing was the caller. Henry would get up on center stage and call out so professionally that he was a sight to see.

Bill and Tomas were your common wall flowers. Every once in a while, Bill would go outside the barn and have someone sample his whisky. By the end of the night many of the young men had gotten a sample of whisky and were feeling pretty loose. Before you knew it two of the young men were grappling outside trying to show who was stronger than the other. In a spur of a moment the grappling turned into a fight. Good thing they were related because the family members were able to break them up. The next morning Henry woke up with a terrible headache. Manuelita wasn't too happy with him.

"You smell like whisky, como *borracho*, like a drunk, if you continue to find ways to get whisky I'm staying home and you'll have to go to the barn dances solito, by yourself!" exclaimed Manuelita. "Now Henry I'll need to get the pay check next week, because you have no sense when it comes to saving money!"

"Andale *chumba*, (short, chubby lady) you know that you love the *baile* (dance),"joked Henry, as he swallowed two aspirin for his splitting headache. Here's to my little lady, bucha, bucha... (kisses, kisses)

"Okay Mr. Barnyard caller you must be the best, joke, joke," said Manuelita as she fed little Juan.

Just then Eduardo Chacon walked into their cabin. "Good morning my brother and sister, are you almost ready for church? Father Antonio is in town and is introducing the new priest who will be visiting us from Denver," said Eduardo.

"Give us a little time. Please go into the other room and get Lucy and Gene ready and I'll get little Juanito. Hopefully, Henry can get himself ready after last night's *pedo* (drunk). We should get to church in plenty of time," said a frustrated Manuelita.

The family went to church that morning by way of Model T; the Henry Chacon family was so excited about their new auto. There it was parked in front of their cabin. It was two toned in color. The main body of the auto was black and the fenders protecting the wheels were ivory white. The front and back bumpers were made of pure chrome and the wheels were pure gates rubber with gangster white walls made in Denver. They were able to get this beauty from the Villanis for a mere $150.00. Henry got behind the wheel while Eduardo got in front of the vehicle and cranked the shaft rod to get the auto started. It was a sight to see, Henry behind the wheel, Eduardo in the passenger seat, and Manuelita with Lucy, Gene and Juan all on her lap.

Back at Bill and Tomas' secluded cabin, production was at full flow. They were producing 100 gallons a day of Canadian made whisky Fountain style.

Many of the patrons of Bill and Tomas made secret arrangements to buy this illegal whisky.

"Just like you said Bill, we are going to become very rich men," said Tomas.

"See, you worry too much Tomas, all along I knew that this would be a big hit. Now all we have to do is sell this product in the surrounding areas, like Carson, Pueblo, Colorado Springs and Security. The key is that we need to make this operation as discreet as possible, kind of like the "black market" that you hear about in New York City, instructed Bill.

"Oh public, but yet private, oh I see," said Tomas.

"You have to remember that if the customer is caught buying the whisky, they too can be arrested and it will be a federal offense," warned Bill.

The two men continued to cover every step they took, making sure that they wouldn't get caught. They wanted to quit working at the mill, but knew that if the business became a bust they would need to continue to make a living somehow. This was truer for Tomas because Bill already had an inheritance from his family in Canada.

The Chacon family finally made it to Holy Mass. As the people were entering the church, Father Antonio Garcia was introducing his brother who'd been visiting from Denver. His brother too had been a war veteran from World War I, like Tomas. The difference between Jose and Tomas was Jose was a Staff Sergeant and Tomas was a Private First Class. Tomas was honored with a purple medal and Jose was honored for bravery in front line battles. Jose was still in the military and now that the war was over he was studying law and someday he'd be a trial lawyer. Father Antonio was so proud of his younger brother. At the end of Mass he asked Jose to tell a few stories about World War I. The congregation was so amazed in what he had to say, that many of the younger men asked how they could join the military. Eduardo Chacon was so interested he made plans to join the service and made arrangements through Jose with the military recruiters in Colorado Springs.

"Someday I too will be able to share stories about my experience as a military man," said Eduardo as they entered the Model "T" on the way home.

"We will all be very proud of you little brother, said Henry. But we will also be very worried about you."

"There will be nothing to be worried about big brother, our Lord will always be there to protect me, I have strong faith," replied Eduardo.

Later that afternoon, Eduardo was invited to Billy Jones' birthday party. The people invited were friends from the mill, all about his age. Billy had been in communication with Tomas and Bill and happened to secure two gallons of their vintage hooch.

"This is going to be one heck of a party," said Billy, as he pulled out two gallons of whisky from his bag. Would you like to try some moonshine Ed?"

"I don't really know Billy, I really try to avoid the illegality of purchasing and intoxication of moonshine," replied Eduardo.

"Oh come on Ed why are you acting like a pansy, a little bit won't hurt," enticed Billy.

The night was very festive. Juanito Vargas brought his guitar and they sang songs to the early hours of the morning. The moonshine supply was dwindling and then Tomas showed up with two more gallons of whisky. Everyone was intoxicated. Eduardo staggered all the way home in hope to find his family's cabin. He found his way home and made it to his bed without Juan Chacon waking up. The next morning Henry drove by to pick up Eduardo and Juan to go to work.

"Wake up little brother; it's time to go to the *trabajo,* job!" shouted Henry.

"Wake up son it's time to go to work, Delfinia has made us quite a breakfast so get up!" shouted Juan. "There's no time for your little jokes, so wake up!"

"Everyone surrounded Eduardo's bed. Let's just throw a glass of water on his face, that will teach him to drink the night before the day he has to work," Henry said jokingly.

Henry then grabbed a glass of water and threw it in Eduardo's face. There was no movement. "Eduardo, Ed, wake up!" They continued to move him and call out his name, but no response…Eduardo…EDUARDO! PLEASE WAKE UP!"

Henry then went over and put his ear to Eduardo's chest to hear for his heart beat, but no beat, no breath or movement. "Call a doctor someone please get a doctor my little brother, my little brother, mi hermanito"

By this time the entire neighborhood was aware of the Chacon's distress. Beto Dominguez the next door neighbor immediately went into town to get Dr. Smith and in minutes Dr. Smith arrived and tended to Eduardo. The entire family was in the front room on their knees praying the rosary and asking God for a miracle. Minutes later Dr. Smith came out of the room with the saddest look on his face.

With tears in his eyes Juan asked, "Is my son going to be okay?"

"I'm sorry Mr. Chacon, I have terrible news, and your son is dead, said Dr. Smith. I'll send in the coroner and let him examine the body and you'll have to make arrangements with Father Garcia and the people at the cemetery."

"Well doctor what is the cause of death, and how did he die?" asked Henry, as he wiped the tears from his eyes.

"Right now I'm going to say influenza, stomach flu, but I have some inclination towards alcoholic poisoning. I'm getting the impression that someone is selling some hooch in this community. This is the third case of influenza or alcoholic poisoning in the past two weeks, informed Dr. Smith. Whoever is doing this is poisoning our youth. Mr. Chacon and family, I'm sorry that it had to be Eduardo. Eduardo had so much potential and is very young.

All of the Chacons and Durans were in deep grief. Eduardo Chacon was the center of the Chacon's happiness. He was the glue that held the family together. Henry was probably the most affected by Ed's death. All Henry could do was think back to the special days that he and Eduardo had spent in Trinidad as sheepherders. The days when they worked the coal mines at Primero and how he suggested the sign from La Virgen to marry Manuelita. The Chacon girls were devastated by his death. All you could hear was an eerie high pitch of crying from Eloisa, Delfinia and Pimenia. Henry and Manuelita were prostrated on the floor and were sobbing out loud.

Henry cried out loud, "my little brother, my brother…"

Juan was in complete shock and couldn't believe this tragedy. "Why Lord, why Lord? This is not fair, he was a good son."

On the way home Henry cried out and sang with sorrow.

"Oh Eduardo, Eduardo what makes you so fat? A piece of cornbread and the tail of a rat… I'll miss…you my brother… I love you hermanito…"

Henry had some idea that Eduardo was poisoned with the bad whisky at Billy's party, but he never pressed charges and never brought it up. Henry never really dealt with it; he just never associated with Bill and Tomas again. The following week people from Pueblo came in to Fountain to purchase whisky from Tomas and Bill. Rumor was that these men were involved in organized crime. Chencho was a witness to a shooting during this time. Two weeks later Jose, Father Antonio's brother was revealed as an informant who actually was an undercover F.B.I. agent who busted Tomas and Bill for producing and distributing whisky. Tomas was tried and convicted and spent nine years in Fort Leavenworth Federal Prison in Kansas. Bill was deported back to Canada. Chencho and the entire Duran and Chacon families uprooted and made their way to Denver to seek a new life and again in history tragedy triggered change in their lives.

El *patron (boss)* of the mill, Antonio Villani was so distraught when he heard the news about the Chacons and Durans leaving Fountain, to go to Denver, Colorado. Manuelita really liked Fountain and wanted to stay there to raise Lucy, Eugenio, and little John. She never understood what killed Eduardo and never knew that Chencho had witness a killing. Henry knew that this would be the best thing to do. So the decision was to exit and start a new life.

"Good bye my friend, I will miss you, your great personality Henry and your very productive work, and this goes for all of you. This also goes to all of the Durans too, I'll miss you," said Antonio as the families left Fountain.

"Gracias mi amigo Italiano, we too will miss you. You were always so kind and gracious, vaya con Dios," said Henry as he gave Antonio a big hug.

The families packed their autos with as much as they could. Then they were on their way to Denver. The families never looked back and cried all the way to their destination. They mourned for Eduardo and their home in Fountain. Moments later, Manuelita could not hold back the news.

"Enrique, this is what she called Henry when she had something serious to say. "I have some good news for you," said Manuelita as she turned to Henry with tears in her eyes, I'm with child again."

Henry looked in his side view mirror and then said, "a child, child, this new baby will bring new life into our new home in Denver. This can only be a sign from God," cried Henry, "this can only be a great sign that God is with us. Let's pray a rosary and ask La Virgen to bless our plans."

The family prayed a rosary on their way to Denver and intermittently would pause to cry, as their deepest thoughts were of Eduardo...

Chapter 9

Denver

The bottle is barren...But life begins...
Tears of despair now become tears of joy...
Hope instead of hopelessness...
Joy instead of sorrow...
Its pungent smell has faded and the aroma of the air
becomes sweet...
Its golden stamp has given its approval...

The Year was 1922 and Colorado was at a point where growth was progressive. Coloradoans had just passed a bond of $6,000,000 to improve highways. All main highway travel routes were made of concrete and gravel. So the way for migration was made somewhat easier. Colorado instituted its first commercial radio station to be licensed and a Federal Reserve Bank truck was robbed as it left the U.S. Mint in Denver. A whoppin' $200,000 in five dollar bills was stolen.

"Mama, where will we live when we go to Denver?" asked Lucy.

"Don't worry mi hijita your Uncle Chencho has made all the arrangements. We will live somewhere on the west side of Denver, assured Manuelita. I trust that your Tio will find us a safe place to live. In no time you'll go to school. I'll have a job cleaning homes, while your Dad will be working in a farm near our home."

Denver was quite a different environment for the families from Fountain. Even though the Chacons and Durans relocated to the west side of Denver where there had been farming areas, the reality of being in the big city was unfathomable and in short, culture shock. The adjustment was quite difficult. The new move meant that everyone would have to chip in and make ends meet. The demands of the big city would include higher rent and more money for groceries. Felix and the rest of the Duran siblings moved in with Henry and Manuelita and the kids. So imagine how crowded it was.

Lucy was six years old and ready to start school. Pimenia stayed with the children while Manuelita worked cleaning homes with Eloisa, Delfinia, and Jesucita.

"Manana, Luz will be going to school for the first time, so tomorrow must be a special day for all of the familia," said Manuelita with a tear in her eye.

"Don't worry my Lady, little Luz will do just fine," assured a confident Henry.

"The greatest and most convenient thing is that the primary school is only a block away. She'll be able to come home for lunch and there will always be someone here to help out with these *chamacos*, (small children)" said Henry as he stuffed some tobacco chew into his left cheek.

Manuelita was very fortunate in finding a job. After Mass one Sunday, she was able to connect with some of the women of St. Cajetan's. The family called the church San Cayetanos. Maria Guzman was her main contact. Manuelita was so fortunate that Maria was able to find her a job a block away from their home. The Radihoffs owned a mansion which needed cleaning. Mrs. Radihoff was a very strict employer. She expected Manuelita to wash and wax the kitchen floor on her knees every day. No ifs ands or buts. This was a daily routine that Manuelita hated and felt that it was a quite a waste of time. Washing and waxing weekly was sufficient in her mind. This was just a small part of her daily routine. She was also expected to wash the dishes, clothes, clean all indoor and outdoor toilets, dust and polish all wood furniture and prepare lunch for Mr. Radihoff. Then after her exhausted day, she would have to run home and feed her familia. Manuelita had been working for the Radihoffs for about a month, when one day Mrs. Radihoff gave her some specific instructions about the day's work.

"Now Manuelita, I'll be gone for the rest of the day. Mr. Radihoff will be here and will need to be fed at noon. Make sure that his meal is kosher. Remember, no dairy products and meats will be eaten together. You know where all of the kosher items are located and don't forget," said an authoritative Mrs. Radihoff. "Patrick and I have business uptown at the Tabor Theatre, so I won't see you until tomorrow. Don't forget my instructions." Then Mrs. Radihoff sped off with Patrick the butler/chauffeur in her new Model A.

The day was somewhat pleasant without Mrs. Radihoff nitpicking every move Manuelita made. So Manuelita made herself somewhat comfortable and put on the radio and listened to her favorite radio station. Before you know it Manuelita was dancing the Charleston, a very famous dance of the Roaring Twenties era. She was a sight to see. She'd shake her little 4'9" body to and fro and then she would grab her knee caps and weave them inside and out. This went on for about 5 minutes when she realized that it was time to make Mr. Radihoff's lunch. During the preparation of lunch Mr. Radihoff walked in and commented on Manuelita's excellent work around the house.

"Manuelita your floors are spotless and the food you've prepared is so delicious!

Has Mrs. Radihoff offered you a raise in pay?" asked Mr. Radihoff.

Manuelita answered, "No she has not sir."

"Well I'll have a discussion with her to give you extra pay," assured Mr. Radihoff.

"Thank you Mr. Radihoff," said Manuelita.

"You can call me Ivan," said Mr. Radihoff.

Two hours had passed and Manuelita was just about finished with all her work. Her last task was polishing the upstairs bedroom bureau. As she bent over to polish the last two bottom drawers she felt something stroking her back. It just happened to be Ivan. In a split second Manuelita stood up quickly and whipped the rag around and hit Ivan's face. She then darted into the kitchen. Ivan grabbed her by her ankle and Manuelita crashed into the kitchen table. Ivan jumped on her and with a flurry of punches she was able to glaze Ivan and scratched his nose. She worked her way from underneath him and then he chased her and tried to make more advances, but to no avail, she was able to make her way to the kitchen door. She ran out the door as fast as she could and in a moment's time crashed through her front door which was a block away. She was totally out of breath. Henry had gotten home early and was so concerned about his young wife. She wouldn't tell him what had happened. It wasn't until two days later that she revealed the truth to her husband.

The next day Manuelita did not show up to work. Mrs. Radihoff was concerned about Manuelita's absence but never felt it necessary to find out what happened to her.

"It's funny how all of these Mexican maids never last for us," said Mrs. Radihoff.

"You must be working them too hard my love," said a romantic Ivan Radihoff.

"Ivan my love, where did you get that scratch on your nose?" asked a curious Mrs. Radihoff.

"Oh I had a disagreement with a rose bush while gardening in the backyard, those rose bushes can be vicious, joked a facetious Ivan.

Meanwhile, at the Chacon residence, Henry was very upset with what had occurred at the Radihoff residence. He went to the local police station to report the incident. The police said that they would look into it, but never did. Two weeks later, Henry and Chencho saw the Chief of Police and Ivan at a local barber shop getting their hair cut. Ivan and the Chief of Police were best friends. The absurd thing about the whole thing was that Henry and Chencho were not allowed into the barber shop for outside the barber shop was a big sign that said, white trade only no Mexicans allowed!

This was the first of many incidences where the Chacons and Duran met up with severe discrimination. They were good enough to clean toilets and pick vegetables, fight for our country in World War, but they were not good enough to have their hair cut at the local barber shop. But, history tells us that our people were survivors

In one scenario little Lucy befriended a young girl Linda in their neighborhood. They were both in the same grade and walked to school daily. Linda and Luz became like two peas in a pod. They were always together. One day on their way to school they passed a synagogue. Here lived a young man, who sat on a swing outside his house on the porch. His name was Horace. Each day as the girls passed his home he'd yell out obscenities. "Go back to Mexico you greasers." The girls were so frightened by this man's indignity. They got smart and reported the incident to the Principal. The Principal said that he'd report it to the police and not to worry. So the girls were assured and never said anything to their parents. Each day as the girls went to school and came close to Horace's home; they would cross the street and then cross back over when they were in the clear of Horace.

Horace was not stupid, just perverted. One day he waited for the girls three houses from the synagogue and hid behind a tree. As the girls walked and giggled to school, Horace jumped from behind the tree and grabbed the girls' arms and pulled them into the abandoned synagogue.

He spanked them on their rear ends and asked why they went to the police. The girls were so scared that they promised that they would not tell anyone. So Horace released them making the girls promise that they wouldn't go to the police. Instead of going to school that day they ran home. When they got home Tio Chencho was there and after he heard the news he wanted to kill Horace. So after he settled down he went down to the police and filed a report against Horace. Again the police said that they would look into it and investigate. Two days later, the police said that they couldn't do anything about it because a neighbor reported that the girls were trespassing. After Chencho got this report he was enraged. He promised that justice would prevail.

Chencho was a very nice uncle to all of the Lucy's siblings, they loved Chencho. To see Lucy hurt made Chencho hurt deep inside.

"How can I get back at Horace, for this injustice?" said Chencho. "I will set up a plan, and justice will prevail."

So Chencho set up a plan. For days he'd been watching Horace's daily routine. Every night around 7:30, Horace would go to the local drug store to buy an ice cream cone. This night would be one of vendetta. Chencho followed Horace from a distance and made sure that no one would follow him to the drug store. Horace stayed inside the drugstore longer than usual. It seemed like eternity, but finally the pedophile would be captured. When Horace came out and no one was around, Chencho followed for some distance and when Horace reached the alley Chencho grabbed Horace by the back of the neck and slammed him into the wall. Horace came up swinging, but could not see Chencho's face. Chencho pummeled Horace until he got him on the ground and commenced pounding him until Horace's face was filled with blood. Then in an instant he cried out for mercy.

After the ass whoopin', Chencho said in anger, "If I ever hear about you spanking any innocent children, I will kill you, do you understand, do you understand?" demanded Chencho. "Remember this goes for any child in this neighborhood, any child, freak!"

Two days later the girls walked to school with confidence and with no fear, for Uncle Chencho walked by their side. Horace was not to be seen again. No one knew where he'd gone.

"Tio, do you think that you can walk us to school every day?" asked Lucy.

"Maybe not every day, because I have to work, but now and then," assured Chencho. "Now if this Horace ever is outside calling you names let me know as quickly as possible."

The Chacons never heard from Horace again and the rest of the time they lived on the west side. They encountered some discrimination, but not as severe as the episodes with Horace and the Radihoffs.

The rest of the days in Denver were somewhat peaceful. The most exciting news was that Manuelita was with child. She gave birth to Maria Rosalia on February 28th 1923. She was later known as Auntie Rosie. Henry continued to work for a local farmer and in the winter he survived by doing odd jobs here and there. Then, after the birth of Rosie the Chacons and Durans made their way north to work for the great sugar beet corporation. Their next home would be in a small town called Peckham, near La Salle.

Chapter 10

Peckham, Colorado

Culture is determined by three aspects; language, customs and religion. Even within cultures we find differences. The key is to respect those differences.

The year was 1924. The Chacons made their living now as farm workers. Henry was given 100 acres of land to farm. Share cropping was his new livelihood. Potatoes and sugar beets were his main crops. A little bit of green jalapeno chilies, a chicken coop for his daily fresh eggs and of course a milking cow. By this time the rest of the Durans moved to La Salle about five miles north down the road. Lucy was now a young 9 year old. Eugenio was 6, Johnnie was 4 and Rosie was now the new kid at several months of age.

Sharecropping was a system that became popular in the United States after the Civil War. This system of farm tenancy was once common in some parts of the United States. Many farmers would hire people to develop the land in turn for a place to stay and a place to make a few bucks to survive the year. Many farm owners had ample land but little money for wages. Because the United States was in a time of progression, land owners would hire people like Grandpa Henry who did not have a whole lot of education but who had the desire to contribute in feeding our country during post World War I times. Grandpa Henry brought to the 100 acre farm only his family's labor. The farm owner or landlord brought to the land, animals, equipment, and seed and would also advanced credit to meet the living expenses of the Chacon family. Most croppers worked under the close direction of the landlord, and he marketed the crop and kept accounts, all Henry had to do was find enough help to get the job done. The labor force for Henry amounted to Manuelita and their children; because they were too young, Henry made use of the *Braceros* (Mexican Immigrants with work permits). Chencho and the rest of the Durans found themselves in a similar situation, working or cropping for other land owners up north.

Now the Braceros primarily worked in agricultural areas of the United States. Small farmers and large growers alike employed Braceros in Arizona, California, Colorado, New Mexico, and Texas. Braceros provided manpower during peak harvest and cultivation times. The Braceros were very hard workers and because the United States was in great need of labor the Braceros would come to work for very cheap wages. The Braceros who were hired by Henry were part of the pre- Bracero Program or also known as the proto Bracero era. The official Bracero Program did not occur until World War II when there was a greater need for cheap labor.

The Braceros who worked for Henry were from the Mexican State of Chihuahua. Their Spanish dialect was somewhat different than the Spanish language the Chacons and Durans spoke, but the communication between patron and worker was clear. They worked and they got paid. The most interesting point was that they were more specifically, Tarahumaras, a distinct indigenous group of Mexican Indian descent. Every night before they went to bed they would go through a ritualistic litany of chants.

One evening, Lucy and Eugenio decided to take a walk by the Bracero's cabin. The Braceros had just finished their chanting, when Lucy heard, "dame *el chicote*' (whip), dame el chicote, give me the whip."

"Gene, Johnny did you hear that?" "Hear what," they said. "Someone who sounded like Dad's voice shouted out dame el chicote," said a frantic Lucy.

"We didn't hear anyone," said the boys. "Well, let's check it out," said Gene.

So Gene and Johnny went over to the Braceros cabin. The men were fast asleep.

"No, it wasn't them," said Johnny, "let's get back to the house."

So the three walked back to the house and found Manuelita there praying a rosary.

Manuelita said, "Look what your father did, he took the horse and buggy, but forgot his *whip* (chicote).

Lucy was totally freaked out. "I knew it; I knew it," said an emphatic Lucy.

"But your father left at noon and you heard the voice this evening?"

asked Manuelita. "Lucy, now go into your bedroom and pray to your guardian angel and he will console you! Make sure that you make this prayer a habit."

Now by the time Henry had gotten home the children had fallen asleep. Manuelita had shared the story with Henry. Henry felt that the advice was great.

"We all need more prayer," said a wise Henry.

The next day Gene had walked by the Braceros cabin. Geronimo the eldest of the Braceros was practicing his English. He kept saying get me the whip; get me the whip, and the voice sounded just like Dad's. He had mimicked Henry's voice to its perfection. Every once in a while he'd say in Spanish, "dame el chicote, dame el chicote." And because Henry spoke very loudly, Geronimo would speak loudly, he was a great impersonator. Gene was in hysterics he couldn't believe his ears. He sounds just like Dad. Gene couldn't tell Lucy about the new impersonator on the farm so he kept the joke to himself.

The next day Henry came into the farmhouse and pulled out his harmonica. He started singing to little Rosie, "Oh Rosie, Oh Rosie what makes you so fat, a piece of corn bread and a tail of a rat? Oh Rosie, Oh Rosie What makes you so fat, a piece of corn bread and a tail of a rat?"

Rosie would get up and dance and sang along with her dad. This was the ambiance that consumed the Chacon home. The other children would sing along. Johnny would pretend to play a guitar and Gene would get the wash board and Lucy would clap her hands as she would dance a jig.

Manuelita was so proud of her family. She sat at the kitchen table and just enjoyed the moment. It was the moment she lived for, happiness and joy. In the corner of her left eye, a tear drop formed and sprinkled down to the table. Little did they know that the news that she would announce to Henry that night was that again, she was with child.

Now, the stay in Peckham was short lived. The next year farmer Andrew asked them to move to Milliken to the Jack Redman Farm, about 10 miles west of Peckham. The Braceros went back to Mexico and now the adventure would continue. The important thing was that they were all together. Home was when they were all together. Peckham marked the beginning of a series of moves as migrant farm workers in northern Colorado.

Chapter 11

A Nomadic Life

...Many times I ponder, for life can be a mystique. To understand my heritage can be quite a feat. Asian nomads are the farthest back recalled. To see those primitive travelers, you might be appalled. Mayas, Aztecas and Toltecas knew the secret to civilization, to settle down, not mess around and forget about migration...

Since the time the families left the Trinidad area, they lived a life of a nomad. This is someone who belongs to a group of people who moves from place to place in search of sustenance. It seemed, when they got some roots underneath them, it was time to pick up all their belongings and head on to the next farm house. The year was 1925. The town was Milliken, Colorado. The Henry Chacon family again made another transition and it was to the Jack Redman farm, outside of Milliken. The work was general farming and some ranching. The most noted thing about this next stay was that Jack Redman and Henry Chacon became very good friends.

Early that spring Manuelita was carrying a heavy load. The pregnancy was a hard one. Manuelita could not deliver her child with the help of a midwife; a doctor had to be called in. That morning Henry sent the other four children upstairs while Jack Redman the farm owner went into town to get a doctor. Lucy was in tears and feared for her mother's life. During the time Manuelita was in labor, all she could hear was her Mother screaming from the intense pain. So Lucy got down on her knees and prayed that her mother and the baby would be okay. Doctor Radovich came in a rush and immediately knew that the baby was breeched. He brought out his forceps to maneuver the baby in a safe delivering position. After fourteen grueling hours of labor, little 9 pound Jim Eduardo Chacon was born. Jim was a name that Jack Redman gave him because Henry was indebted to Jack for paying for the doctor. Jim was Jack's father's name who'd died a year earlier and of course Eduardo came from his little brother who'd died several years ago in Fountain. But everyone called the new little brother Eddie.

The stay at the Jack Redman farm was short lived for by the next spring the Chacons found themselves in Colorado Springs in a small farm outside of the city. It seemed as when Henry heard about a new opportunity the family picked up and took their belongings to the new place of opportunity. Then a year later, the call back to northern Colorado was in Henry's ear. The stay was just that, a stay and off they went back to northern Colorado to a small farm near the town of Eaton at the Henry Swanson farm.

Lucy, Gene, Johnny and Rosie will always remember the Henry Swanson Farm, because this where they met their great grandparents Francisco and Dolores Duran from Trinidad. The Chacon's had special visitors from Trinidad. Great Grandpa Francisco was a brilliant story-teller. He was able to keep the attention of his grandchildren in the most loving way. Manuelita hadn't seen her Grandfather and Grandmother since the days they lived in Trinidad. She was so happy. When they found out that Manuelita was ready to give birth in the next upcoming months, they insisted on staying and helping the family until the new baby was born. The evenings were the best time to hear Francisco's stories. After Henry's long day of working on the farm, the family would gather around the kitchen table and find ways to entertain themselves. Henry was good with his poetry and music and Francisco was great with his legends, fables, and myths.

"Come on *abuelito* (grandfather) can you tell us a story please?" asked an excited Lucy.

"Si mi hijita, I'll tell you a story, answered Francisco. "Well the story goes something like this; once upon a time there was this great big country. This great country was known for its great wealth, the richest country in the world. The unique thing about this great country was that it had a humongous garden. Not only did this great country feed itself from this giant garden, but also it fed the world, todo mundo! This great country had all the plants that you could think of, potatoes, beans, squash, carrots, radishes, beans and cucumbers to name a few. Included in this giant garden was also an orchard with all the fruit you can think of and corrals filled with animals ready for slaughter, pigs, cows, and chickens. But the one vegetable that stood out in this giant garden were the big green jalapeno chili peppers. The chili peppers are what gave that needed flavor to make all combinations of food, superb tasting," explained Francisco. "These peppers were the spice and secret to all good eating." Francisco continued, "One day there was no more green chili, no more *chili verde*. Could you believe? The chili had all been picked. All foods were bland and had no flavor. The great country was in turmoil and slowly lost its greatness. Mysteriously enough, other countries became great and this one great country was now weak and feeble."

"Now children could you imagine eating beans without chili?" asked Francisco. "Of course not, it would be so plain that when the flavor is lost everything is a disaster.

"How about potatoes, without chili, eggs for breakfast without green chili, what a fiasco life would be!" "Where am I going with this story my little and big children?" asked Francisco.

Henry raised his hand up slowly and asked, "Do these vegetables, fruits and meats represent people?"

"Yes Enrique, you are headed up the right path. They all represent people, the people of this great country. And we the migrant, represent the big green jalapenos who add spice to life, who give flavor and is the missing piece for our country's great success. Could you imagine this country without people like us? History, time and time again has taught us that the migrant, the worker, has built great things, like the Pyramids in Egypt and Mexico and now the great Panama Canal, emphasized Francisco. We are the backbone of this country but yet we have to continue to travel like nomads looking for our next draw of water. Our kind, are survivors, my children, survivors!"

Henry sat there in awe and couldn't believe the story that came from this little man. Francisco was truly brilliant. How could a man have so much knowledge without any formal education? Was Francisco's fable trying to tell Henry it was time to settle down?

The very next morning Manuelita was experiencing labor pains. Everyone in the household shouted, the baby is coming, the baby is coming." Great Grandma Duran was right by her side. "Now mi hijita this will be number six for you so it should be an easy delivery, but we have to be prepared for the unexpected," said great grandma in a calm voice. Eddie was a hard one but I believe that this will be much easier."

Later that morning, Manuelita's water bag busted and two hours later a grappling 6 pound baby girl was born. This was the beginning of a great legacy for this grappling little baby later in life became my mother.

"What shall we name her?" asked Gene.

"This is going to be a very special one." said Henry, "we'll name her Maria Candelaria. That's my mother's name," boasted a proud Henry. "For short, we'll call her Lala. *Siguiéremos adelante con una vos así clara, el nombre de su hermanita es María Candelaria.*"

From this point in little Maria Candelaria new life, Henry knew that his Lala would have a beautiful and clear voice. His expression valued the beautiful voice she would have. He made this clear to the children that she would be a singer.

That evening before nightfall Francisco concluded the night with another fable.

"Now tomorrow Grandma Dolores and I will be on our way to visit the other grandchildren in La Salle, so before we leave, I'd like to leave with you another story, *un proverbial* (proverb)..."

Many years ago there was a small village. In this village there lived two men who called each other compadres. One was *Curioso* (curious) and the other was the other was *Tramposo* (tricky). The Compadre Tramposo was always trying to get the other man in trouble.

One day compadre Tromposo decided to sell his burro to compadre Curioso. Tramposo told his wife, "I guess I am going to sell my burro to my compadre!"

His wife replied back, "I don't think he'll buy it from you."

Very upset with what she said, Tramposo explained, "Well this is what I'm going to do!" "What are you planning?

"Are you upset that this is not one of your tricks?" his wife questioned.

Tramposo answered, "I plan to put $10 into the burro. Every time I poke him in the ribs he'll let out a $1. Then compadre Curioso will think that he will get rich."

The next day, he went on his burro to his compadre's house. Tramposo asked Curioso if he wanted to buy the burro, but the compadre said no! Curioso didn't think he could afford it.

Then compadre Tramposo said, "Compadre! You don't know it but this burro can make you rich. Look, all you have to do is get on him and poke him in the ribs and he'll let out dollar bills."

So Curioso got on top of the burro and he poked the burro's ribs. Then out came a dollar and then two dollars until all ten dollars came out.

Compadre Curioso saw how true it was and told Tramposo "Oh yes compadre! I will buy the burro from you. How much are you selling it for?" Tramposo replied back, "Give me one thousand dollars!" Compadre Tramposo left with the money and was extremely happy. After all that is what he wanted. He went home and showed the money to his wife.

"Look at all the money I got from selling the burro! We are rich!" Tramposo yelled at his wife.

His wife yelled back and said, "That's not fair!" Compadre Tramposo explained, "Compadre was satisfied with the burro. You should have seen how delighted he was when I sold him the burro."

The next day compadre Curioso came over and he was very upset. He told compadre Tramposo that the burro was not letting out any money. You have tricked me compadre and I am going to take you to jail. "Compadre," Tramposo said, "Don't worry." I will go over to see what I can do. Go home and I'll be there tomorrow."

That night he had to think of another idea to get money from his compadre, so he killed a goat and got one of the intestines and filled it with blood. He then told his wife, "when tomorrow comes I will put this gut around your neck and then I will cut the gut and Curioso will think that it is your throat and you will fall down on the floor like you're dead. I will get the trompetita (little trumpet) and I will make him think that I can bring you back to life. So I can get my trompetita and say, "Trompetita, trompetita, trompetita, revive my wife, three times and on the last time I say trompetita you start to move until you finally stand up."

The next day compadre Curioso got tired of waiting for compadre Tramposo to come over so he went to Tramposo's house madder than before. "Compadre, you promised to come over but what happened?" "I couldn't go because my wife wanted me to run some errands." At that time the wife walked out.

She said, "Don't lie. I didn't do such a thing." They then began arguing. Compadre Tramposo jumped up and cut her throat. She fell down dead on the floor.

Compadre Curioso said, "You killed your wife! What are you going to do?"

Compadre Tramposo said, "Don't worry. I can revive her with my trompetita." He took the trompetita and put it up to his mouth and began to say, "Trompetita, trompetita, trompetita revive my wife." Then on the third time, she started to move and she stood up.

Compadre then said, "You see, you can kill your wife and revive her with this trompetita.

You saw it happen. You saw it all." Poor Compadre Curioso forgot all about the burro and compadre Tramposo tells him to see this is a good thing to have because you can kill your wife and bring her back to life with this trompetita.

Compadre Curioso says, "I suppose you want me to kill my wife."

And Compadre Tramposo said, "She won't die. You saw it all."

Compadre Curioso says, "Please sell me the trompetita. I need it. It will teach my wife not to say so much." He brought the trompetita and gave another thousand and compadre Tramposo was happy. Now he had more money. The next week Curioso came over real mad and told him that he had killed his wife and that it was his fault and had come over to drown him in the ocean.

Compadre Tramposo said, "Yes I think it is fair." So compadre Curioso put him in a gunny sack and started his trip to the ocean. When he was real far he had to pass by a church and he said, "I can't go by without going into the church to say a few prayers." Compadre Curioso saw a lady sweeping the patio and he asked her to do him a favor and take care of the sack until he visits the church and says a few prayers.

The lady says, "Of course I will take care of the sack." While she was sweeping she heard a voice telling her, Abuelita, grandma!" She heard the voice coming from the sack.

He asked, "Do you have something to put in this sack, because I will be drowned in the ocean if you don't help me."

The lady said, "I have a cat that just had kittens that I want to get rid of." So she put the cat into the sack and tied it. Shortly, came compadre Curioso, who took the sack and thanked the lady and was off to the ocean. On his way he heard a meow that sounded like me me me and said, "me meow you are going to drown soon. And as the proverb goes, Curioso killed the cat. Or as the proverb states, curiosity killed the cat.

So you see, my loving grandchildren, I leave you with this story. Curiosity has its limits and the key is not to be to nosy, but be aware of what is around you. Please don't believe everything that is told to you, it can get you into grave problems.

This was my Great Grandfather Duran's rendition of "curiosity killed the cat." It has some semblance of the original by Ben Jonson a British Playwright from the year 1598. Being too inquisitive can many times get a person into as Francisco said, "grave problems."

Little Lucy was very much taken by this proverb, so she went into her bedroom and wrote the story of Compadre Curioso and Tramposo. Later Lucy memorized the proverb and shared it with all of the neighbors and cousins who would come to visit.

The stay in Eaton did not last too long. It's like one would have their suitcases half emptied before it was time to leave to the next farm. Henry was always looking for opportunities. In the next year and a half they found themselves in Laporte near Fort Collins by the Poudre River where he worked in the cement plant and then off to Severance where they worked at the Henry Swanson farm.

Today Severance is known for serving the best Rocky Mountain Oysters in Colorado, but then it was where number seven would be born; Verlinda Manuelita would be born on September, 25th, 1929. Verlinda would be the last child born to survive from Henry and Manuelita. The time after Verlinda's birth proved to be a trying time for Manuelita.

Chapter 12

A Liberated Woman

Amendment nineteen, gave women the right to vote, the right of citizens of the United States to vote shall not be denied or abridged by the United States or by any state on account of sex. Could you imagine, Women could not vote until 1920?

Manuelita was ahead of her time when it came to technology. Henry had taught her how to drive the family's model T. Few if any women during this time drove. So one day when Henry and the older boys Gene and Johnny were out doing field work for Henry Swanson, Manuelita was up and about driving the T. She loved to drive the T.

"Now Lucy, I have to go to La Senora Swanson's to share my pies. Get your brother Eddie, and sisters Rosa, Lala and Verlinda, I need you to bring them into the house, feed them and after lunch, nap time."

The year was 1929 and Manuelita thought of herself as quite a driver when it came to driving the Model T. She needed to be at Mrs. Swanson's home at noon "Lucy I'll be back after 1 o'clock so you have do all the jobs I've asked you to do, said a hurried Manuelita. Lucy immediately went outside to gather the children into the house.

"Lala, Rosa, Eddie get inside, it's time for lunch!" yelled out Lucy.

Lucy gathered all of the children in, but she could not find Lala. At that very instant, Manuelita with her hands holding two apple pies came running out of the house, jumped into the car and backed up with a sudden urgency. Then, long and behold Lala's curly brown head poked up from under the car. She was under the car playing in the dirt. When Manuelita caught glimpse of Lala, she stopped the car and screamed out with such ferocity that even Henry, who had been working at a near field came running with such speed, Jim Thorpe would have been left in the dust. When Henry got to the scene Manuelita had Lala in her arms.

Henry, cried out, "Mi niña! Mi niña! Que paso, con la Lala?"

He made his way to the scene with tears running down his cheeks. Gene and Johnny came moments later, also with tears in their eyes. "My sister, my sister," cried out the boys.

Manuelita barely missed running over Lala. There was such a great relief to see that Lala was okay. Manuelita repeatedly said that she would no longer drive the Model T or any other motor drawn vehicle till the day she died.

Who knows if La Senora Swanson got her pies, but it didn't matter to Manuelita and the Chacon family for Lala survived the terrifying moment. Afterwards the Chacon family went in front of the family altar and recited a rosary and thanked God that Lala was okay. From that point on Manuelita made sure that all of her children were accounted for.

I don't know if Manuelita ever voted. The process for a woman to vote was a slow one. But all I know is that she took a risk and was one of the first few women to drive in 1929.

Chapter 13

The Henry Swanson Farm

One early spring morning, Henry Swanson called a meeting of all the workers on his farm. The meeting was so important that other important people from the great sugar beet industry were present. The subject at hand was the production of sugar from the sugar beet. That morning Henry took out all the men to the field and demonstrated the process of planting, growing and cultivating the sugar beet. Henry Swanson was an articulate and educated farmer who had gone to college and his expertise was not only in the field but he also had book knowledge. That morning he stood in front of his workers and corporate bosses and made the most eloquent presentation.

"You see the sugar beet business is like one big cycle," started Jack with his dissertation. "The seed is planted in early spring. We use a beast of burden-drawn, four row beet drill."

As Henry pointed at the machine he said, "Make sure that you plant a lot of seed; this assures that the seed will grow. In early June the seed will take hold and germinate. Now, when the seed develops four leaves it's time for thinning; now for you Mexican and Spanish speakers that's called *desaihe.* Now how do I know this, well I spent many years in Texas and the Tejanos down there taught me a lot of Spanish. Now don't think that you can call me all those bad words amigos, because I know them all," said Jack jokingly.

When Henry Swanson laughed his face turned beet red, please forgive the pun. He was somewhat over weight and when he laughed his sides giggled like jelly. He was a sight to see.

"Subsequently the field is blocked by cutting out plants in rows with a hoe so that bunches of plants are evenly spaced about eight to ten inches apart Next, thinning of bunches by hoe removes all weeds and 'lo and behold' one plant. Then the plant grows and matures and the plant is cleaned from all weeds. This is called the cleaning or the *limpia*. Then the field is furrowed and prepared for irrigation and cultivated with a machine to keep the dirt around furrows loose," emphasized an exhausted Henry.

"After that, late in late September we'll plow and cut the tap root, loosen the dirt so the beet plant will be pulled out easily. Then with long knife you'll top the beets by cutting the leaves from the beet. Next, you'll load the beets into a wagon ready for delivery to the beet factory to make sugar," concluded Henry.

"Now Mr. Wilson my boss, would like to say something to you," introduced Jack.

"My endowed and committed workers, the success of this company is dependent on you. You are the back bone of America. You, feed this nation," said a patriotic Mr. Wilson. "Now go and share this news with your families and tomorrow you, yes you will make history as we compete with other nations and become the bread basket of the world."

Henry Swanson then called Henry Chacon over to interpret into Spanish what Mr. Wilson had said.

There had been a sense of nationalistic pride spread throughout the Henry Swanson farm. Henry passed the information to Gene and Johnny and emphasized the part about how their job was so important, that he only expected the best from his sons.

"Now my sons, it is now a matter of doing our best with these sugar beets. No slackers, just hard workers," said a proud Henry Chacon.

It seems as if this was the big push, to motivate all of the small farm owners in the area. So this sense of pride to feed our world was propagandized throughout America. The whole idea was that we were in competition with other countries to grow and have the best product no matter if it was fruit, vegetable or livestock. In this case it was the sugar beet.

Americana or the culture of the United States had hit the Chacon Family. They were proud to be Americans. When The fourth of July came around the Chacons were there celebrating with their American flags. Their cars were adorned with all of the usual hoopla of the holiday. When it came to the fourth Henry Chacon would take his family to the Weld County Fair in Greeley and afterwards they returned home to Henry's firework display. Not only did his family enjoy the fireworks, but also all of the *vecinos*. (Neighbors) But sad in their celebration the Chacon progeny were not allowed to trade in certain businesses in town because of the color of their skin. "White trade only" signs were displayed in Greeley, Fort Collins, Loveland just to name a few. Sometimes this rejection from their fellow Americans could be so humiliating that the Hispanos would have to find ways to survive. This gave birth to the Spanish Colonies in Greeley and Fort Collins. These were little shanty towns where the Hispano Farm worker would live if a farm home was not provided by the farmer. In any case most living conditions were poor. Sanitation was up to the family who lived in these shacks. Manuelita was a very clean woman and always made sure that cleanliness was next to holiness. These colonies were refuge for these workers. Many times the local store would serve as a place where groceries and hardware could be bought on credit. In the city there were some stores who would trade with the Hispano farm worker but few, as the practice of "white trade only no Mexicans allowed" was common. Another way that the Hispano farm worker would identify was their membership in clubs that were loyal and patriotic to the United States of America. This organization was called, American Citizens of Spanish Descent. In many scenarios the Hispanics who were born in the United States and had a long lineage in the United States were vehement to let everyone know that they were Spanish not Mexican and foremost Americans. Nonetheless, it didn't matter to the anti-Hispanic businessman if you looked Mexican you were not allowed to trade and if you spoke Spanish it was a sure thing that you could not enter. It was like the old Jim Crow laws in the south after the Civil War. We are probably more familiar with, "Separate but Equal." When you had separate facilities for whites and separate facilities for people of color. A great example of this was when one day Henry Swanson invited Henry and Gene Chacon to view a matinee in downtown Greeley.

"Say Henry and Gene would you two like to go see that new Charlie Chaplin flick, *The Immigrant*, I heard that it was really funny? It's showing at the Kiva theatre on 8th street, here in Greeley" entailed Henry Swanson. "We've got all of our business done and now it's time to relax and have some clean fun." Gene was truly thrilled and couldn't believe his ears as his father said ok, let's go.

Now Henry and Gene Chacon didn't know that the Kiva theatre in Greeley practiced the separate but equal policy. But Henry Swanson was a very affluent and well known man in the Greeley community. When entering the theatre, the proprietor immediately told the Chacons that they would have to sit in the balcony. When they were told this they looked back at Mr. Swanson and he told them, "just ignore them you can sit on the main level with me, to hell with their intolerant and ignorant policies" Henry Swanson retorted.

During the movie the Chacons were stared at but Henry Swanson continued to say ignore them we are having fun and no one will ruin it for us. Gene never experienced so much fun in his life. He was in heaven enjoying his buttered popcorn, soda and juju beans all paid for by Henry Swanson.

After the movie they went home. Gene told the story to his mother and siblings. "Mom you should have seen us over at that movie theatre. Dad, Henry Swanson and I we were all sitting in the white peoples section on the main floor and no one made us sit in the balcony, said an excited Gene." Here are some juju beans for the rest of the kids." All of the kids gathered around their big brother while Gene passed out the candy.

What could have been a humiliating experience in the balcony became quite gratifying for Henry and Gene with their bags of popcorn and boxes of juju beans.

Chapter 14

Opening a Restaurant during the Great Depression, were they out of their Minds?

The year was 1929 when America gave birth to its new child, "The Great Depression." The Stock Market crashed and the whole American economic system went out of control. People began to congregate in soup lines hoping to get enough food for their family's sustenance. Money had very little value and poverty was running rapid, especially in the bigger urban areas like New York, Boston, and Los Angeles to name a few. Would Denver be impacted?

Ironically, during this time in America's depression, Henry, Manuelita and their compadre Juan Madrid opened up a restaurant at their new business location at 23rd and Larimer in lower downtown Denver. Why lower down town? Well the answer was clear. You go where you feel welcomed. In this case Henry chose this area because of the large population of Hispanos, like himself. Apparently, Henry, Manuelita and Juan saved enough money to lease their own restaurant. Rumor had it that Juan was a popular bootlegger up north and that's why he left northern Colorado to invest in this new business and most likely to hide from the law.

Being comfortable in a new neighborhood was important and this lower down town district would be the place to get rich. Like the colonia in northern Colorado this neighborhood would be perfect to cater to the people and their delicacies for Manuelita's great cooking, plus it was a good hide out for Juan.

Now Manuelita's new occupation was quite different for her. Instead of just cooking for the whole family, she now was conjuring up a menu of her favorite delicacies that would meet the wants and desires of lower downtown community. *Pastel* or pies were her specialty, not to exclude some more of the traditional foods of the southwest. Twenty third and Larimer was not their residence but 33rd & Julian on the northwest side of Denver. The northwest side of Denver was primarily populated by Hispanos and Italians. The new neighborhood school would be a challenge to Lucy and Gene. Fairview Elementary was their next place of learning.

Now, while Henry, Juan and Manuelita were trying to get rich during the Great Depression, Gene would have to deliver the newspaper downtown.

"Gene, make sure you make it to school after you sell the newspapers!" warned Henry.

"Don't worry about me Dad, I'll make sure that I get my education and get rich at the same time," assured Gene.

Now one day Gene and Mr. Rossi, a diminutive man in stature had been delivering newspapers for the past 20 years met at 16th & Glenarm. Mr. Rossi gave Gene some specific instructions on where he could sell and not sell news papers. Rossi stood at 3'11" and had the biggest moustache a man could have. His voice was deep and loud. It sounded like a great baritone booming in the Grand Canyon. So when Rossi spoke people listened. He'd been selling newspapers in downtown Denver for the past 20 years.

"Now Chacon, I'm going to make this clear to you, do not sell newspapers on 16th and 17th street! This is my beat. You can only sell on the corners of 14th and 15th streets. Do I make myself clear?" As Mr. Rossi instructed Gene. Then with a haughty look, he pulled a Cuban cigar from his front shirt pocket and put it in his mouth.

Gene replied quickly, "yes sir, yes sir."

Now Gene was a stubborn kind of fellow, he too, like his dad looked for opportunity to make a quick buck. A week went by and his area to sell papers was somewhat slow to sell the newspapers. On Friday of that week, Mr. Penny who ironically worked at J.C. Penny's on 16th street, asked Gene to sell him his bunch of papers. He made this requisition so he could have papers available for his customers at his store. Gene felt that this would help him get to school in plenty of time and still make a quick buck. Gene was elated and never had to worry about selling on the corners of the streets.

As the weeks passed Mr. Rossi's sales were going down. Times were tough for the Rossi family, it was the depression! He was so upset about his loss in sales that he started to investigate the problem. He noticed that there were many people reading newspapers at the trolley car stops and wondered where they were getting them from. Finally, he asked several people and they said that they were getting the papers at J.C. Penny. Why J.C Penny? So Rossi continued his investigation and confronted the manager of the store.

"Excuse me sir, my name is Rossi and I'm responsible for selling the newspaper in this area on16th and 17th streets. Who is selling the paper to you? I need to know because it's hurting my sales."

"I'm sorry sir, but Mr. Penny has made all of the arrangements with a young boy who works over on 15th street, a Mexican boy with real dark brown straight hair and slicked back," replied the manager. "Tread lightly, because Mr. Penny likes this kid and just wanted to give him an opportunity so he could make it to school on time."

After hearing this Mr. Rossi was livid. He wanted to kick the shit out of Gene.

"I'll just wait for him in front of J.C. Penny and then the fight will be on. I'll whip him like I'm his daddy," said an angry Mr. Big Man Rossi.

So that next morning Gene in his merry way was off to deliver his bunch of papers to Mr. Penny. When Gene was about a block away he saw Rossi with his sleeves rolled up and was bantering back and forth in a boxing stance. He saw Gene and started shouting you little, jive turkey!" Rossi's voice was booming like an m-80 firecracker on the fourth of July.

Gene at age 12 was very scared and was always taught to respect his elders so when he was confronted by Rossi he tried to explain what Mr. Penny was doing. Now the scene was quite funny to see. Rossi with his diminutive stature of 3' 11" taking swings at Gene was quite hilarious. Gene would hold out his right hand and placed it on Rossi's forehead while Rossi tried to punch him. Gene would not dare hit him, so when Rossi slipped down to the ground he left Rossi in the dust as he ran off.

This ended Gene's career as a newspaper man. He would have to go help out with the business at the 23rd street Café. His days of getting rich would have to wait and now his education would be first on his priority list.

Meanwhile, at the restaurant after several weeks, the business went broke. The impact of the depression was apparent, also in Denver. People could not even afford to buy a piece of Manuelita's delicious pies. So after a short time Henry would have to migrate again, back north to pursue another financial opportunity.

23ᴿᴰ STREET CAFÉ MENU

Proprietors- Henry Chacon and Juan Madrid
Featuring pies by Manuelita

Entrees

Hamburgers – 5 cents
Cheeseburgers -6 cents
Bowl of red chili (Chile Colorado) - 5 cents
Bowl of green chili (Chile Verde) -5 cents
Calabasitas (corn and squash) – 3 cents
Fried potatoes – 2 cents
Tacos – 3 cents
Bowl of Menudo – 5 cents

Desserts

Pies – 2 cents per slice

Coconut Cream	Peach
Lemon Meringue	Empanadas/peach/lengua/apple/pumpkin
Banana Cream	Apple

Chapter 15

A Singing Career
1935

Many years had passed since the Chacons migrated back from Denver. The children were growing up fast. After the experience of turning down two proposals of marriage, little Lucy was now Mrs. Daniel Apodaca. The Walter Lewis Farm was their new residence and the new place for educating the kids was Smith School. Gene was sixteen and was preparing for entry into the C. C. camps at Estes Park. Johnny was 14 years old and was finishing up his eighth grade year at Smith School. Rosie was a 12 year old and practicing her jokes and songs. Eddie was 10 and getting his education. Lala was 9 and Verlinda was 7.

Henry was now 40 years old and Manuelita 36. They had done a great job in educating and motivating their children to love music and entertainment. It was quite by accident how Maria Lala Chacon discovered her new talent. Rosie, her older sister had been practicing duets with her friend Dora. Lala was quite the nosy young girl and wanted a part of the action. So daily, she would listen to them practice singing in the kitchen. Then, she would go and rehearse in the bathroom. The bathroom was an ideal place to practice. The sound effects were comparable to a microphone and an amplifier. She was nine years old and Verlinda her younger sister was seven years old, when they started singing duets. It seemed very easy for her to give harmony to her sister's melody. Lala was quite a talent in her young age, for not having any formal vocal training. She never studied in an elite school of arts, but practiced daily with her sister and brother

Johnny who also was a tremendous talent. His guitar playing was beyond compare. Corridos, wampangos waltzes, and ballads were Johnny's forte when it came to music.

Johnny seemed to always be the center of all entertainment at home and school. One day while in class, Johnny had a severe stomach ache from eating too many *frijoles* (beans) the night before. So randomly, he'd let out gas (silencers). The classmates were very uncomfortable with the smell. Johnny just went along with the class and said that it sure reeked and that someone should shoot the person who was farting. Johnny got away with that one and always seemed to find ways to make life fun. Johnny also was the entertainer out in the fields. When the work got hard and grueling, he would do impersonations, jokes and sing songs both Spanish and English. He was hilarious!

"Mama now that I'm a man, *un hombre,* I would like to go out and sign up with one of those government programs that President Roosevelt has developed, they're called the C.C. camps," said a very patriotic Gene as he waved the application in front of his mother's face. "C.C. means the Civilian Conservation Corps, this brochure says that I will help develop America and it all starts in these Rocky Mountains to our west. This program is designed to plant trees, combat soil erosion and build reservoirs. It also gets rid of stream and river pollution. Finally, it creates fish and wildlife sanctuaries and looks at the minerals that are being deposited into the streams. Doesn't it sound exciting, Mom?"

"Mi hijito what does this mean?" asked an inquisitive Manuelita. "Does this mean that you'll be going off and never coming back, like at war."

"No Mama, It's just a job to help build up America and give jobs to those who are struggling during this Depression. It's a great honor to help build up our country," said a proud Gene. "Anyway Tio Matias and I have been talking about this for quite some time." He wants to bring in extra money to support his familia."

Gene pulled out the application and filled out all of the information. There was one line that he was having problems with, the date of birth. In order to work at the C.C. camps one had to be 18 years old. Gene falsified the records and wrote in that he was 18. Now all he had to do was take it to the Department of the Interior in Fort Collins. Also in the application one had to be single. Tio Matias was married, but yet he too falsified his application and said he was single. Times were hard, so many would do anything to try to bring money to the household, even if it was criminal.

"Now how are they going to know that I'm 16? They're not asking for a birth certificate or any form of identification," said an introspective and excited young patriot. "Now if I get accepted, what would I be able to do with the money?" Gene thought to himself for a second. I could buy myself some new clothes and possibly buy Mom and Dad a new truck, which would be nice.

So the weeks went by and the Chacons waited patiently to see if he would be accepted. Daily, Gene would walk to the post office to see if the government letter would come. Gene had just graduated from grammar school several years earlier and wanted to make money to help support the family. Henry would use him as much as possible at the farm. If it wasn't plowing the fields, it was running the routine of the sugar beets. It was Gene's dream to leave the migrant routine and venture off to independence. Then, finally in June, Gene received his letter.

"Dad, I finally received my letter. I didn't want to open it until I got home, so we will all get the news together," said an enthusiastic Gene. "Ok everyone; it's time to open it."

All of the familia gathered around the kitchen table and then Gene opened it. "Look everyone, an official document from the government."

Gene read carefully the letter and at the bottom of the letter it read, you Eugenio Chacon have been accepted. After Gene read those words he let out a shout and then immediately there was a silence in the room. Everyone looked over to their mom and noticed that tears were profusely streaming down her face.

"Okay it says here that I have to report on Monday morning at 10 am and my assignment is Estes Park, wherever that is?"

Gene then proceeded to go through all of the information. In the information kit he found a map of Colorado and an illustration of all of the sites that would be developed by the C.C.C. And of course a personalized letter from President Delano Roosevelt.

"Look Mama a letter from the President, said a comforting Gene, Mom everything will be fine. I'll work for 3 months this summer and then I'll be back and then we'll have a great big fiesta, alright, Mamacita, alright? Anyway you can also go up and visit."

Manuelita could not hold back the tears. So to comfort her, Gene gave her a great big hug, *embrazo*.

"Andale Chumba, our hijito is a man now and we must respect his ambition. Anyway, he'll be back. The map shows that he'll only be 45 miles away, he'll be close. I guarantee it, my little *vieja* (old lady)," said a joking Henry.

Early that Monday morning the entire family drove to Ft. Collins where Gene would get on the bus to Estes Park. Everyone gave their goodbyes and Gene was on his way. On the way home no one spoke a word. All you could hear was sniffling of noses and some sobbing from Manuelita and the girls. Henry tried to be strong but soon as he made it back to the farm he let out some tears for his oldest son as he went behind the barn. He then went back to the house and instructed Johnny that he would take over all of the chores that Gene did and he expected him to step it up in his production in the beet fields. Johnny assured his dad that he would try to meet all of his expectations. Then he instructed Eddie that he would take over Johnny's chores.

Meanwhile, on the trip to Estes Park, Gene was very quiet and only spoke to the young campers who spoke to him. The road to Estes Park was not quite developed and the ride was very bumpy and at times treacherous, especially when they went through the Big Thompson Canyon. Gene could not believe the beauty of the sierra before his eyes. It was awe inspiring for sure. He could not believe that he was away from his family who he loved deeply. There has to be a first time for everything he thought and now it's my turn to see if I can change this routine that our family has lived through since the beginning of time. It's time to get off the farm and have our own independence from the farmer. Our country is the land of milk and honey and now I want to be free as a bird and provide for myself. I want a piece of the economic pie! But that night all Gene could do was hold back the tear. Good thing that it was dark inside the tent or everyone would have made fun of him.

Back home the Chacons would pray a rosary daily for the safety of Gene. Working in the *sierra* (mountains) could be a very dangerous job. So when it came to prayer the Chacons kept the tradition alive. La Virgen would keep him safe.

The Chacons kept themselves very busy at the farm. But in terms of entertainment, the family loved to party. Henry's affiliation with the American Citizens of Spanish Descent was strong. Their upcoming festivity would be a talent show in Greeley at the local radio station. This was going to be a big contest and not anyone could compete, you have to be invited. I'm entering la Lala and la Verlinda for the competition. I'm an officer and I have that privilege! It's called officer prerogative.

"Okay Johnny, I'm assigning you a big task," said Henry. "You are going to prepare Lala and Verlinda for the competition. I believe that they are going to win."

"Okay papa I'll give it my best. What songs should we play?" asked an inquisitive Johnny, as he bent over to grab his guitar.

"To appease our Spanish and Mexican population we'll sing, Maria Elena and for our Anglo population we'll sing Elmer's tune." That should convince the judges, I hope," said an excited Henry.

So daily, the three would practice until the songs were perfect. The Chacon sisters had somewhat of an advantage over their competition, for their music teacher Miss Curtis caught wind of this competition and made sure that the girls and Johnny would practice in the music room after school. It seemed as if she was just as excited as the Chacon youngsters.

The next morning Lala was so excited to get to school early. So she grabbed her lunch quickly from the kitchen pantry. You see Manuelita was very thrifty and made use of everything she had and made sure that she didn't waste anything. She always packed the children's lunch in an empty Rex lard can. So that morning Lala grabbed a can and was off to school. When it was time to eat lunch she went off to the lunch room with Chela her best friend and sat at a dining table.

"Say Lala what do you have in the can for lunch?" asked Chela. Your Mom makes the best lunches, especially her *pasteles*, her pies?"

"Well let's see," responded Lala, as she grabbed the can.

As she opened the Rex lard can all she could find was white creamy lard. Lala brought the wrong can to school and felt so embarrassed.

What made matters worse is that Chela shouted out, "Look Lala brought lard to eat for lunch."

"Shut up Chela, shut up, you are embarrassing me, shut up!" yelled out Lala.

Lala wanted to crawl into the can and thought to herself, no wonder why they call us Mexican greasers. She wanted to pound on Chela but couldn't because of the ridicule. So later, her brother Eddie gave her a piece of tortilla to eat to hold her over until she got home.

When Lala got home she was famished. Manuelita was waiting at the door with the can with her real lunch, the good stuff. Lala told her mom what had happened. Manuelita thought that it was hilarious and couldn't stop laughing.

Meanwhile, back at Estes park Gene was having a hard time acclimating. It seemed that Gene was the brunt of many jokes. Because he hadn't been anywhere in his short life, the other campers loved to make fun of his inexperience. When it came to being educated in the world he was quite naive. One day the other boys decided to play a joke on Gene.

"Hey Gene we are in need of fresh milk, take that milking bucket, go down to the barn, down the road and bring us some fresh milk," said Ted the camp leader.

"Okay boss," shouted out Gene.

Gene went out to the barn, grabbed the bucket and was on his way. It was twilight and the night was drawing near. Most of the other campers were strolling in from their job sites. Gene was like a salmon swimming upstream.

"Work is over with for the day Chacon, it's time to go to the mess hall to grub," said a hungry Tom Jones, a new friend of Gene.

"Oh I was instructed to get fresh milk from the milking cows in that barn down the road. Come with me so I can do this right," said Gene.

When Gene and Tom entered the barn there was only one bovine present.

"Now let's get the rope and put it around the cow's neck," said a determined Tom.

Gene made a nice loop and threw it around the bovine's neck. Then the cow turned around and started to charge Gene. Gene ran as fast as he could outside the barn into the corral. Tom shouted out, "Gene you've been duped, the cow is not a cow, but a bull!"

Gene and Tom could not stop laughing. Gene then had a great idea, "let's buy a quart of milk put in the bucket and fill the rest of the bucket with water, they'll think that I accomplished the task, but the joke will be on them."

When they entered the camp the camp leader was waiting with a big grin on his face. "Chacon did you get the job done?" asked Ted as he smirked and laughed.

Then Gene poured out a glass of milk for Ted. Gene then turned to Ted with tongue in cheek and said, "Now that's a bunch of bull."

Everyone turned to one another and then there was an uproar that echoed throughout the canyon.

Back home the Chacons continued to practice for the talent show, which would be aired on the radio station. The other students in the class heard about the Chacon's debut at the radio station. They all gave their 'good lucks' and 'I hope you wins' before they went home that Friday after school. There was one kid who was very jealous and thought that Lala and Verlinda were terrible, his name was Wesley Howard.

'Why are you competing?" asked Wesley. "You sound like a bunch of coon dogs howling for their next meal. You have no chance. You might take last place!"

"Thanks a lot Wes, that's your opinion and everyone here, except for you say that we're going to win that competition," said a confident Lala.

That next morning Manuelita took out two very beautiful dresses that she had been working on for months. They were both pink with ruffled sleeves.

"Good morning *mis lindas* (my beauties), the other contestants don't stand a chance against you two beautiful princesses," said a confident Henry. "Johnny you make sure that the guitar is tuned and then we'll be on our way!" shouted Henry as he swallowed the last bites of his breakfast.

The drive from the farm to the radio station was about a 20 minutes. The radio station was located off 8th street and 10 avenue, near a drugstore. This is where Henry bought the girls and Johnny some penny candy for after the competition and a cherry coke before the competition to loosen up their vocal chords.

When they got to the radio station they were asked to take a number and go back to a room to practice. One by one the contestants went into the recording studio to perform. After each performance the contestants were asked to come back at 2pm to find out the results.

As the time drew near the Chacons were very nervous. Finally, the Chacons were announced. The three went into the recording room and were asked to sing and play directly into the microphones. Then they were announced to the audience in radio land.

"Straight from Severance Colorado we have the Chacons, singing melody is seven year old Verlinda and giving her harmony is nine year old Mary Lala and accompanying them on guitar is older brother Johnny, take it away," announced the radio jockey.

The two girls looked at each other and then Johnny counted out, "1 2 3 -123." They started with Elmer's tune and their harmony was perfect. Then they sang Maria Elena. Again the song was sung to perfection.

Back home all of the neighbors were near their radios and were hoping and wishing for the group to win the competition. Even Wesley Howard's family sat near their radio.

"Listen Wesley, do those girls and their brother go to Smith school. Do you know them?" asked Mrs. Howard.

"Yes mother, Lala is in my class at school," responded Wesley.

"They sound like professionals. Are you sure they go to your school?"

"They've got my vote for the best act so far," said Mrs. Howard.

Wesley then remembered what he told them on Friday. "They do sound pretty good. I'll have to eat some humble pie come monday," thought Wesley.

After the competition Henry and the children went across the street to Lincoln Park, also known as the 'Chili Bowl' by the Spanish and Mexican community in Greeley. This is where the American Citizens of Spanish Descent set up a booth so people could read all the literature about the civil rights organization.

"Did you know that there is a change in the agenda?" said Ernesto Garza president of the organization. The radio jockey Tom Morgan is going to come out to the park and announce the winners."

When 2 o'clock came the crowd started to gather around the gazebo in the center of the park. Everyone's eye was on the door that just opened across the street at the radio station. Out the door came Tom, as he made his way slowly to the park with ribbons and a list of the winners.

"Good afternoon my fellow northerners," greeted Tom Morgan. "Today is a great day for us as we honor our local talent. The competition was fierce and for those people who did not make it to the final 3 there is always next year. Now for our finalists we have some special prizes for 3rd place the prize is a $25 gift certificate to Ben Franklins. For 2nd place the prize is a $50 gift certificate to Gambles Dry Goods and for 1st place a $100 bill donated by an anonymous donor and a chance to make a record at KNCO Radio Station."

"Let's give a round of applause to our first contestants, placing 3rd from Ft Collins Colorado, Benito and Margarita Montoya."

The Montoyas came up to the gazebo to receive their award. Benito gave a small speech thanking all the people who made it possible for their success. He was so grateful that he started crying, from the joy in his heart.

Tom grabbed the microphone from Benito and thanked him for his speech.

"And now from our neighbors from Cheyenne Wyoming, in 2nd place is Los Misquez in their rendition of Paloma Blanca and the Silvery Moon," announced Tom.

The crowd gave their applause and Manuel the father of the group graciously accepted the award. Manuel had been the reason why Johnny was such a great guitar player. Several years prior Manuel had taught Johnny how to play.

The Chacons waited patiently as Tom announced the final winners. "And from Severance, Colorado home of the World's best rocky mountain oysters, in first place, Los Chacones, Johnny, Maria, and little Verlinda. Let's give them a round of applause."

The crowd immediately stood up and gave them a standing ovation...

"The crowd chanted *Otra! Otra*! (Encore! Encore!)" Then Mr. Morgan called the trio up on stage and they sang Elmer's tune.

After the song, Mr. Morgan handed Henry a hundred dollar bill. Henry then, gave a heartfelt speech, thanking the audience for all their support.

The funny thing was nothing was said about recording a record. Wasn't that supposed to be a part of the award? Who knows? Henry never investigated the non compliance. So life went on. The Chacon sisters later sang at several September 16th celebrations and Fourth of July festivities at Island Grove Park and all that mattered was that they were great singers with no agent and promotion.

When Lala got back to school Miss Curtis announced the Chacons had won the competition. All of the students stood up and gave them a standing ovation.

After school Wesley Howard walked up to Lala and said, "You know Lala you sang pretty darn good on the radio. You didn't sound like a bunch of coon dogs. My Mom thought that you would be the champions, congratulations."

Wesley humbly walked away and started running toward the playground. Lala sure felt good hearing this from the bully of the school.

"Thanks Wes! Thanks!" shouted Lala.

Meanwhile, back at Estes Park Gene found himself at the main office of the C.C. Camps and Officer Wagner was asking Gene some pretty confidential questions. You see some where through the rank and file the administration found out that Gene was only a 16 year old and he lied about his age.

"So Chacon you want to join the trucker's union? Well I have some bad news for you, you're fired! We found out that you are only16 years old," said an emphatic Officer Wagner. "You know Chacon, this is a serious offense, lying and falsifying government records is a federal offense. According to the law you can serve a year in juvenile hall and many hours of community service. But because you did such a great job building this camp, we're just sending you home," said a stern Officer Wagner.

"You see sir I did it for my family," pleaded a scared Gene. "We are migrant farm workers and we needed the money to survive these hard depression times."

Gene then tried to hide the tears.

Officer Wagner got him a cup of cold water and said, "Chacon tomorrow your bus will take you back to Fort Collins.

"I apologize for any wrong that I did," said a humbled Gene as he walked out the building.

The drive home was a long one. Gene had lots of time to think. He thought to himself, "What will I tell my parents? What will I do now? Now I'll have to go back to the fields. I tried to do something right and it all turned out wrong. Will Dad punish me? What is my alibi?"

Henry waited patiently that next day for his son in Fort Collins at the Department of the Interior building. When Gene got off the bus he thought that Henry would be very upset, but quite the contrary. He was very happy to see his son.

"Gene you should have discussed this matter of lying about your age with me. Now your record will be tarnished and you will not be able to get another government job," said a very concerned Henry while he gave his son a great big hug.

"Dad you're making me feel like the prodigal son all over again," said Gene as he wiped the tears from his face. "Where are Mom and the rest of la familia?"

"Eugenio! You ask too many *preguntas* (questions) mi hijito, as Henry laughed putting Gene's entire luggage in the car.

"You will get to see them shortly," assured Henry.

The two jumped into the car and down the road on the north side of Fort Collins was a park. Gene said, "Look Dad, that looks like Johnny and Eddie playing in the park. It is, and all of the girls Verlinda, Lala, Rosa, they're all here and Momma too. What a blessing, thanks Dad."

"We all missed you so much, so we planned a picnic for our prodigal son, our lost son has been found." said a very happy and forgiving Henry.

Chapter 16

School House Bullies

1936 became a very trying year for the Chacon children, especially Lala. The family made another move and their new residence was a small farm right outside of Windsor called the Westerdahl Farm. Lala now was in the 4th grade, Verlinda the 2nd, Eddie the 6th, and Rosie the 8th. Gene and Johnny were full time workers for the farmer in Windsor. Lala's name was now Mary. You see her name was changed. It's called forced assimilation. You know the routine. Miguel became Michael, Juan became John, Eduardo became Edward, Rosalia became Rose and Verlinda became Verlin. These were all good American names. These were names that the teacher's could pronounce. The goal was assimilation, and throughout all of America people's names and cultures were being changed. The Spanish language in the classroom was forbidden and if you spoke any other language than English you were swatted and sent home. The goal of assimilation was an accepted institution. No one dare challenge its power. The right to be different was taboo in the eyes of some of the new immigrants who came from Europe. So when someone was different they were treated with such degradation that they were dehumanized for their differences.

Carl Greenstead was his name. He had to be one of the meanest kids in the fourth grade. He was already tall for his age. He stood at a lofty 5'6" and had the reddest hair to match his red freckles. Every time he'd speak, he'd drool and spit would land on your face. Carl was a true artist when it came to harassing the other students. He loved to spit in the other student's faces and when the teacher wasn't looking he'd flick your ear lobe. The teacher never found out about his misbehavior because if you told on him he'd threaten to beat you up after school. Everyone was afraid of Carl, especially the Hispano students. His favorite saying was "hey dirty Mexican! You have cooties."

His best friend was Ruben Detter, an overweight spoiled kid who was raised by his grandparents. The Detter farm was the largest beet farm in the Windsor area and many Hispano migrant farmers were employed by the Detters. His favorite put down was "you're nothing but a son of a bitch." Not too many people picked on Ruben because of his family's wealth and influence with the rural community.

As the story continues, Mary, Verlin and Rose always walked to school together and Eddie would walk ahead with his friends who were also of Hispano descent. On more than one occasion the Chacons were subjected to great ridicule just because of their skin color, language and religion. The other anglo kids loved to throw rocks and called them 'dirty Mexicans!' The harassment was very degrading and humiliating. There had to be a stop to this hate crime!

It's kind of funny that a lot of these migrant families found themselves migrating together from farm to farm. Chela Apodaca, Dan's younger sister, Lucy's sister-in-law also moved to a farm near Windsor and again was in the same class with Mary.

"Hello is Lala home, I mean is Mary home?" asked Chela, as she opened the screen door to the farm house.

"Si Chela, un momento, yes one moment, let me get her, said Manuelita. "Have you heard from Dan and Lucy? You know that they were miners and lived in Silt?" said Manuelita.

"Of course Manuelita they're my relatives too. And now they are living with us on the Jessie Evans Farm, *muy cerquita de aqui,* very close to here, responded Chela."

"Yes Manuelita they are doing just fine, I get to see little Beatrice every day, she is so cute, replied Chela.

At that moment Mary aka Lala came walking through the door. "Mary sure that you get the right lunch bucket, now double check, I don't want you to eat Rex Lard for lunch, ha ha ha," laughed Chela.

"Oh shut up Chela, you just can't put that in the past, can you?" retorted Mary sarcastically.

Even though Mary and Chela loved to argue, they actually were very close friends. Everyday Chela would stop by and pick up Mary, Verlin and

Rose for school. Each and every day the children would have to dodge rocks and insults, as they walked to school. The children always learned to always look all around to help protect themselves from any flying missiles. One day when the children were walking to school the girls found some retaliation to the intolerant counter parts.

"Here he comes, Carl with his fancy horse, showing everyone how much money he has, said Rose. I'd love to punch him right on his freckled nose."

"Don't look at him, just ignore him, said Mary.

"Hey, look at those dirty Mexicans, they have cooties all over their bodies, you are dirty Mexicans, dirty cootie, cootie," harassed Carl. "Cootie, cootie, cootie infested Mexicans!"

Then Carl commanded his horse to push Mary into a ditch filled with stickers and weeds. He then sped off as fast as the horse could run. Mary was a quite a sight to see. She had scrapes and a bruise on her legs and a nose that was bleeding profusely and her hair was filled with sticker weeds.

Rose was fuming mad and chased the horse all the way back to the school. Chela and Verlin helped Mary clean up as best they could.

"I'll get that 'son of a bitch,'" shouted Mary.

Mary did not waste any time as she got closer to the school thought in her mind, how she was going to kick the shit out of Carl. In the meantime Rose ran into the school to tell the principal what had happened. She couldn't find the principal so she went directly to her first period class. When Mary arrived at the school, she went directly to her fi rst period class. Carl was sitting there telling all his friends how he knocked down a dirty Mexican. As she entered the room their eyes locked and like white on rice, Mary pounced like a puma on prey and pounded on him while he was in his desk. As she punched she could feel her knuckles crunching the protruding bone on his nose. He was stuck in the desk which made it easy for Mary to pin her victim in his desk. Every time he'd tried to get out of his desk she smacked his face harder. It was quite a sight to see this little girl who had this big kid in a trap and he couldn't escape.

"Mary, Mary, Stop it! Stop it!" said a frantic Mrs. Menca.

The entire school caught wind of the fight. Rose went ballistic when she heard that her little sister was in a fight. She went running from her classroom and darted into the music room.

"Kick the shit out of him, hit him, hit him," yelled out Rose.

Then Mr. Morrison from the eighth grade came into the music room to help break up the fight.

"Mary now, Mary, stop it! Back off!" yelled Mr. Morrison, as he pulled Mary away from the beaten Carl.

Mary stopped flailing her fists and Carl slowly stood up. Carl's face was beet red and blood was coming from his nose.

"Carl, this dirty Mexican just kicked your ass," taunted Mary. You're not as tough as you think you are. A girl just kicked your ass, sissy!"

Mrs. Menca was serving as the principal that day so she took Mary and Carl to the main office.

"Tell me what happened Mary why are you so angry?" asked Mrs. Menca. "Carl called me a dirty Mexican and he knocked me into the ditch with his horse.

Mrs. Menca's murmured, "Well Mary you are a Mexican aren't you?"

Nothing really happened to Carl that day, except for getting totally annihilated. From that point on Mary had a reputation, not only was she an awesome singer, she could also fight with the best of them.

The rest of the year was somewhat peaceful. The walks to and from school were peaceful. Except for one day when Ruben Detter another school house bully called Chela, Mary's best friend a "son of a bitch." Again, Mary was on the war path and caught Ruben walking up the stairwell. Punching and pummeling, she knocked him down the stairwell until he was his backside on the first floor.

"Don't you ever call me or any of my friends and family that name again, or your next beating will be worse," said a sassy Mary Chacon. "Remember what I said!" "Your ass will be mine!"

Chapter 17

A Request for Forgiveness
El Betabelero

Now at age 19 Gene Chacon was a well known beet worker in Weld County, probably the best beet worker in Weld County. In his youth he was getting somewhat restless. The great sugar factory loved to promote competitions within the farms to see which farms would have the most production. When it came to the time of the season to top beets the competition got intense, it was similar to a major contest amongst all the farmers and their workers. Many times the workers were promised great awards for the work they did. Henry always contracted for 11 acres where the common worker would contract for 9. That's how much confidence he had on his family. Of course Gene was the fastest but Johnny at times would give Gene a run for his money. Eddie was still a young boy but was expected to pull his own. Rosie was a speed demon when it came to topping beets. She was so fast that when she got going you couldn't see her hands nor the topping knife. The owner of the Westerdahl farm called her speedy Gonzales. Henry kind of spoiled his two youngest daughters, Mary and Verlin and thought about excluding them from the hard work and just letting them help Manuelita prepare the food, wash clothes and keep the house clean and orderly, but Rosie insisted that they had to work too, no exceptions!

"Dad you can't show favoritism it's not fair. They need to pull their weight also," said a vehement Rose.

"*Bueno,* good then, they'll pull their own weight and work like mules," said Henry. "Sometimes I feel like a slave! But one of these days none of my girls will have to work!"

The Chacons could get product from a field of 5-6 acres a day. So in 2 days Henry would meet his goal and then immediately pick up another contract. So when one deadline was completed Henry was working on the next opportunity. The job was grueling and merciless. Sometimes one would be working in the rain and at other times it could be 100 degrees in the shade. If you were not properly clothed you could get the worse sun burn. If you were not hydrated, sun stroke was inevitable. Yes! Not too many people could do this type of job. How do you motivate someone to do this kind of job? You promote it through propaganda and incentives. In order to promote the incentive of the job, Henry would promise his children spending money for clothes, dances, harvest festivals, trips to Bell Market and the downtown stores in Greeley and Fort Collins.

Bell Market was known for doing business with everyone. Bell market was a very lucrative business. By the time harvest came around, the majority of the farm workers owed all their hard earned money to the market due to the credit built up throughout the year.

The "White trade only" signs were prominent on the south side and downtown of Ft. Collins, but Bell Market, a Jewish owned business on the north side was open to everyone.

The process of promoting propaganda came to telling the children that they were feeding the world and that it was their Christian obligation to fulfill that task. That they were making a difference and if no one knew about the difference at most, God did...

But Gene was getting too restless. His time away from home in Estes Park gave him a sense of independence. Would there be a way off this plantation? Was there life outside these fields? And could there possibly be a beautiful woman his life?

"Enrique, Henry it's time to wake up," said Manuelita as she rolled out the side of the bed.

"*Cinco*, five *minutos mas* my little chumba," mumbled Henry as he rolled out bed.

"*Vieja!* Ole Lady! Get the boys and girls up for breakfast and I'll get the firewood, para la *estufa*" (pot belly stove.)

It was 3 am, the alarm went off and the daily routine of the *betabalero* (beet worker) began. It all started with gathering the firewood to get the stove ready for cooking the breakfast and warming the house. After breakfast Henry would get the entire group and pack them into the back of the pickup truck and transport to the beet field that was going to be topped, cultivated and loaded on the trucks for harvest. Then the beet workers would get out their tools of the trade and work as fast as they could, cutting the tops of the leaves from the beets so the plow would follow cultivating all of the sugar beets. Cool days were ideal, but even in September the sun could blister your face.

It was early September and the harvest of the sugar beet was here. Contracts were being signed and money was to be made. But the routine was very demanding; everything had to be set in place. Lunches had to be made. Water jugs had to be filled and the correct clothing had to be worn; like hats, gloves, boots, etc. etc. The long topping knives had to be their sharpest and the ole body had to be ready to work like a machine. All for $21.00 per acre or as Henry contracted for $1.80 per hour.

One day Gene over heard his younger brother Johnny talking about joining the C.C. camps. The next place to be developed was a place called Ted's Place up the Poudre River. There was also talk about a place called Red Feathers just north of Fort Collins.

In a matter of weeks after cultivation of the sugar beets Johnny found himself up the Poudre River and about 30 miles north at Red Feathers Lakes developing camp sites for tourists.

Oh, how Gene longed to be up in the mountains and getting out of the farming business. This would be an ideal time, because harvest was over and his labor wouldn't be needed as much during the winter months. Gene was so envious of his little brother. Johnny didn't have to lie about his age, so he was legitimate.

"Why did I join that stupid truckers union?" That's the only way they found out about my age, said a very disappointed Gene Chacon. "You know that honesty is always the best policy. I sure wish that I would have been honest and waited until I was 18."

So one day Gene went to the Social Services building in Ft. Collins where he met an old friend of the family, Ray Lopez. Gene shared his story with Ray about how he was fired previously from the camps at Estes Park. Ray was one of the directors of Social Services. He came up with a great idea. He wanted Gene to write a letter of apology to the government.

As a result of this letter Gene was absolved of his offense and readmitted to the camps and found himself working at Ted's Place up the Poudre River developing camping grounds for tourists.

Chapter 18

Love Potion at a Medicine Show.

In the summer of 1939 on a break from the C.C. Camps, Gene found himself at a medicine show on Walnut Street in the northern section of Fort Collins. He had been invited to this medicine show by a good friend of the family, Robert Moore. He chummed around with Gene earlier when they worked in the beet fields.

Featured at this medicine show were a number of music acts, sometimes a Hollywood celebrity would be featured but the focus was the sale of some concoction elixir that could supposedly heal any and all ailments. Many times a market in the town to be visited by the medicine show would promote this medicine show. Bell market was on a big promotion of this show. Gene and Robert saved enough vitamin box tops to get free admission to the show.

"It sure is nice to get in free to this show," said Robert.

"Remember Robert nothing is free, we bought many vitamins to get into this show," said a correcting Gene as he nibbled on some popcorn.

Then the final act came on the stage.

"Hello my name is Dr. Jack Wilson," introduced the Medicine Man as he held up a bottle of medicine up to the audience. "This bottle of elixir has many healing powers. It will cure the common cold, rheumatism, arthritis, tuberculosis, diabetes, hay fever, and many more. But, the most affective power is its power of love. Yes ladies and gentlemen it's a love potion. It will make you appealing to the eye."

"Gene can you believe that, a love potion," whispered Robert. "We will be a hit with all the women, like real gigolos."

"We need to buy a case or two." suggested Gene.

Then at that very moment the medicine man called for a volunteer. Many people raised their hands, but there was this man who was chosen. He literally crawled up on stage with crutches under his arm pits and metal braces on his legs.

"Good evening my friend and what is your name?" asked the medicine man.

"Well, sir my name is Frank Watkins, I'm from Mount Vernon, Iowa. I've come a long way to see if your elixir can heal my crooked spine, so I can walk again. My life has been miserable, I need a cure."

"Frank, I can't promise you a miracle but I've seen this medicine work," announced Jack as he opened the bottle of elixir.

Then from the bottle he poured, he put some of the liquid on a clean piece of cloth and rubbed it all over Frank's legs and back. Frank then positioned himself on his back and slowly took the braces off his legs. On his back he slowly moved his legs in a bicycling motion. He then stood up with the help of Jack the medicine man. Surprisingly, he then stood up and took one, then two steps forward. His wife then ran up on stage screaming," it's a miracle! It's a miracle! Frank and his wife were in total embrace crying tears of joy.

"Ladies and Gentlemen you've heard it and seen it here with your own eyes in Fort Collins, Colorado," said Dr. Jack Wilson, as he held up the elixir.

That testimonial ended the show and then the crowd lined up to buy the elixir.

"Gene do you believe what we just saw?" asked Robert.

"I really don't care about that miracle mumble jumble," said Gene. "All I care about is the picking up of women part," joked Gene.

In minutes the two young men found themselves in line buying the elixir. Gene bought two cases and Robert bought four cases.

"I know that we are going to be a hit as soon as we drink our first bottle," said Gene.

"I agree, let's not waste time" said a confident Robert.

As they carried the cases to the car they joked around about the reputations that were in their future. Then midway to the car Gene placed the cases on the ground and chugged a whole bottle down.

"Hold it, Gene, it says that that you should start with two table spoonfuls, not a whole bottle, pendejo!" scolded Robert.

"That whole bottle will make me extra handsome!" said a conceited Gene.

"We'll soon find out, let's wager," said a betting Robert. "In one week let's see who gets the most babes."

"Okay Casanova, twenty dollars, here's mine, where's yours?" asked Gene, as he pulled the dollars out of his back pocket.

Gene took Robert's twenty spot and put it in his wallet. They agreed that in two weeks, if one didn't have a girlfriend the other would keep the twenty dollars and if they had no girlfriends they'd get their money back.

The two Don Juans made their way back to Robert's car. They both drove to Robert's parent's home, not too far from Walnut Street. When they got there they unloaded the elixir and went into the Moore's home. Gene had met the Moore's previously from the field work. They lived in the city and would drive out to work on the fields during harvest time.

Gene was feeling somewhat strange from the excessive amount of elixir he consumed. Gene asked for permission to use their restroom. When he was in the bathroom, he looked in the mirror and said, "Man! You are one handsome man, Gene. The women do not have a chance."

When he came out of the restroom he saw a beautiful young lady sitting in the Moore's front room. When he looked at the young lady, their eyes locked and then he felt this weird feeling inside. "Wow, is this potion already working? She's really smiling at me, thought Gene. This potion is really making me handsome!

Robert then turned to the beautiful young lady and said, "Gene, I want to introduce you to my little sister Maggie."

Gene reached out to shake her hand and said, "Hello my name is Gene Chacon and I didn't know that your brother Robert had such a beautiful sister."

Maggie then blushed, and said, "Oh you're too kind and sweet."

Maggie's parents were very nice people and talked all night about the good ole days. Then his parents asked Robert to go to the store to buy some refreshments. Gene and Robert went out the front door. Robert's dad insisted that they take Maggie. So then Maggie, Robert and Gene were off to Bell's market to get some refreshments. Robert told Maggie to sit in the back and keep quiet. But Maggie wouldn't stop talking. She was so intrigued by Gene and his experience in the C.C. Camps.

"Say Gene, do you have a lady?" asked an inquisitive Maggie, while Robert was in the store buying the refreshments.

"No," answered Gene as he looked into Maggie's eyes. You have the most beautiful eyes Maggie."

"Thanks Gene," answered Maggie.

When Robert came out to the car Maggie was sitting in the front seat in the middle. He tried to force her to the back, but she refused. On the way back she happened to hold Gene's hand under her coat so Robert wouldn't see. Gene really didn't mind, he thought that she was very beautiful.

Gene hadn't held hands so soft in his life. Her perfume was so sweet smelling and her laugh was like the Sirens in Greek mythology. "Boy does this potion work well. If I was on stage now, I could give a great testimony about my Casanova image which happened minutes after I drank the elixir," thought Gene as he was day dreaming about Maggie.

"What are you daydreaming about Gene?" asked Maggie.

"Oh nothing, I was just thinking about the man that was healed at the Medicine show," answered Gene as he looked at Robert while he was driving. "Yea some guy from Iowa was healed from his crippled condition.

Gene peeked over at Robert and could see that he was not too happy with him and his sister. His face was beet red and every time he looked at Gene he'd give him a sigh of disapproval, like 'oh brother.'

When it was time to go Robert walked up to Gene to say good bye.

"Hey Gene, the bet's off," said Robert as he held out his hand for his twenty bucks.

"It was your idea that we went back to your folks place, replied Gene, and anyway how did I know that that potion was going to work so well, it's your fault. Here's your money!"

It was getting late and it was time to go back to the Westerdahl farm. Maggie came running outside and passed him a note telling him she wanted to see him again. On the drive back he couldn't believe how fast the potion worked. He really felt bad that Robert didn't approve of him flirting with his sister.

A week had passed by and Gene hadn't heard anything from Maggie until one day she showed up at the farm. You see she borrowed the family car to see Gene. They visited each other and then she picked up Gene at the farm and took him back to Fort Collins to tell her parents that they were going steady. Her parents really liked Gene and gave them their blessing.

But the blessing was not mutual at the Chacons; Maggie was a Protestant and the bad experience with Manuelita's Protestant siblings left a bad taste in Manuelita's mouth. This did not set well with Manuelita because about the same time her brothers and sisters, the Durans had converted to the Pentecostal religion. Her oldest brother had swayed her other siblings to convert. This left a deep wound in her heart.

Gene went back to the C.C. camps up the Poudre and kept in contact with Maggie and on weekends they dated.

Chapter 19

A Schism in the Family

A schism is defined as a major split within a religious denomination. This usually occurs when there are differences in beliefs or practices of the dominate religion. The Chacons and Durans were predominately Roman Catholics. The Durans made a decision which caused a division and differences in theology. The Durans believed in the power of prayer through the doctrine of the Pentecostal Religion, where the Chacons believed that God works through the doctors and gives them healing powers through medicine and the powers of the Church, Scriptures and the Holy Magistrate.

The most noted schism in history happened in the 1520's when a Catholic monk by the name of Martin Luther decided to take a stand against the Catholic Church. He wrote his 95 thesis stating all the wrong things the Church was doing. His major complaint was the sale of indulgences, monetary payment to have your sins absolved. His major complaint was that Tetzel the indulgence salesman was traveling throughout Europe telling everyone that they were going to hell if they didn't have their sins forgiven. These indulgences were ways to pay for a direct path to heaven. In reality these indulgences were being paid to pay for the beautiful church at St. Peter's Square in Rome.

After Luther's stand and excommunication from the Church, many northern European countries sided with this protestant disobedience. As a result of the revolt in the north, religious wars took place killing thousands of Christians on both sides of the disagreement. When this debacle seized

Martin Luther, he stood in disbelief and wished that the schism never took place. The papal authorities only wished that Martin Luther's approached would have followed the protocol of the Catholic Church. Some authorities believed that Luther could have been the Pope if he would have been patient and obedient to his advisors.

It's amazing how even in 1939 Martin Luther's Protestant Reformation had a great impact on the Chacons and Durans. Can you imagine four hundred and nineteen years later this Protestant rebellion separated the love between these two strong Christian families?

Oh, how Manuelita loved her Rosary and Catholic Church. As a little girl she was Baptized and dedicated to the Catholic Church and community of Weston, Colorado. Her parents Felix and Gracia loved her so much that they had enough confidence that the Church was the way to the Kingdom to God. Felix and Gracia according tradition invited two friends to be sponsors for their little beautiful angel. They would be responsible for Manuelita if anything would happen to her parents. Then the priest baptized her sprinkling water on her head and said, "I baptize you in the name of the Father, the Son and Holy Ghost."

Manuelita continued her strong belief as a Catholic, practicing the sacraments of the Church, Baptism, Confirmation, Holy Eucharist, Penance and Holy Matrimony. She had a great relationship with Jesus through intercessory prayer with La Virgen de Guadalupe in the Rosary. Her marriage was blessed by a silver rosary. She raised all of her children to be devout Catholics.

In 1939 a schism, a separation in religious practice took place between the Chacons and Durans. Edward Duran, Manuela's oldest brother became one of the first Hispanic ministers in the Pentecostal Church. The rest of the Duran clan followed their brother as he started his church in northern Colorado, everyone, but Manuelita.

She was devastated when she received the news. When this happened she cried for days remembering the days she spent as little girl going to church in Weston. She remembered her mother's funeral, where the priest gave such a beautiful eulogy and how a proud Henry stood up in front of the church so handsome and eloquent at the altar reciting his alabado. "Did my family forget about that and how La Virgen brought Henry and me together?" thought a distraught Manuelita.

Now and then Manuelita would get an invitation to big brother's church in La Salle, but Manuelita refused to visit the church. Many came from afar to listen to Edward's preaching and told Manuelita about how spiritual he was, but to no avail. All Manuelita would say, "That's nice, but my priest's homily is sufficient for me. I receive my Jesus in communion every time I go to the true church."

Edward and Chencho were persistent. They insisted on converting the Chacons into Pentecostals. One day after a long day working the fields, Edward and Chencho along with the rest of the Duran sisters decided to visit Henry and Manuelita in Windsor. It was twilight and Henry and Manuelita had just finished eating supper and then decided to pray the rosary, when Chencho came in and yelled out, "Alleluia, my brothers and sisters in Christ, the lost sheep have been found."

Henry stood up and welcomed them into his home and said, "Before we visit with you, we must have respect to La Virgen and finish Her Rosary. You are welcome to stay and pray."

The Duran clan sat around and started praying, with their alleluias and amens. Henry was offended by the way they tried to proselytize his family. So at the conclusion of the Rosary, Edward pulled out his King James Version of the Bible and began to preach about how the Rosary was repetitive prayer and in scripture Jesus does not approve of this.

All Henry could say was, "if it's good enough for our past generations its good enough for me, so let us be." "Now I would like to ask you to leave, Henry said reluctantly. My wife, your sister can not handle this. Please show respect to our home and leave."

"Henry we will be asking Our Lord and Savior to save you through prayer. We know that you and your family will convert, said a confident Edward as he grasped his Bible. It will be the power of prayer through Jesus Christ, for he is the way the truth and the life."

The Durans left clapping and singing spirituals. The Chacons were so upset, all they could do was stay in the house and pray that the Durans would come back and be who they were before. But Manuelita knew that this would never happen and now they were lost forever.

Chapter 20

Chiropractic or Medical, You Make the Decision

The Chiropractic medical field was founded in 1885 by D.D. Palmer and is now practiced all around the world. Chiropractic has been the subject of controversy, criticism, and outright attacks. It has come from critics within the profession, critics outside the profession and from researchers in the scientific community. In history, these have indirectly led to scientific investigation of chiropractic and an antitrust suit against the American Medical Association. As direct result of this criticism, as well as the relative dissatisfaction with its medical counterpart, surveys show that patients have the highest satisfaction rate among the various healthcare disciplines. (**wikipedia.orgchiropractic_medicine**)

Chiropractic comes from the Greek word chiros and praktikos which means "done by hand" it is a health care profession whose purpose is to diagnose and treat mechanical disorders of the spine and musculoskeletal system with the intention of affecting the nervous system and improving health. In layman terms Chiropractors adjust the spine by manipulation. Some work on the whole body making adjustments by manipulating the spine and depend on organic herbs to heal the body naturally; where medical doctors medically survive by the use of prescribed medicine and surgery. The Chacon's experience with chiropractic came at a very precarious time. It so happened in 1940 when Johnny was 19 years old and terminally ill. He had a terrible cough and complained of a terrible stomach ache. As months passed he lost a total of 60 pounds, from a strong 158 to a 98 pound weakling. Manuelita was frantic. She couldn't believe that her son was dwindling before her eyes. Johnny went to every medical doctor in the Fort Collins and Greeley area seeking a remedy for his ailment. Some doctors believed that he had influenza and others thought he might have a bleeding ulcer. But the general consensus was that he had tuberculosis also known as "T. B." The symptoms of T.B. included of course his loss of weight, no energy, he wouldn't eat, night sweats and he was constantly coughing. All the doctors recommended lots of bed rest and an occasional dose of ether, a liquid gas that was used to stop pain from increasing. Manuelita was in constant prayer asking God for a healing. Her prayer was so strong that one day God came through. Her faith was what got her through the ordeal and belief that Johnny would be whole again, being himself, the ole jokester. So one day she went to Bell's market where she met one of her old friends. She shared her situation with her friend on how Johnny was ill and that he was losing pounds as they were talking. Then this lady sat in contemplation... "Hum," she thought. "My friend, I'd like to recommend Dr. Nather, a chiropractor who healed my lower back problem. He has healing hands and uses different methods than your common doctor." "Is he a curandero, a witch doctor?" asked Manuelita as she had this look of despair."

No she said, he's has doctor's degree from Palmer Chiropractic in Iowa, like I said he's a different kind of doctor."

In a matter of seconds Manuelita found Henry in the store and said, "Enrique we need to go to set up an appointment with this Dr. Nather.

"He has the healing touch to cure Johnny." "So everything else hasn't worked, let's give this chiropractor a try," said Henry.

From Bell's Market they drove to his office and set up an appointment for the next day. When they got home Johnny was in bed, just lying there moaning and groaning. The family couldn't stand hearing him in pain. They all would cry, but not in his presence, so they would show strength. Lala probably was the closest of all the siblings to Johnny. She prayed for her brother and cried and also asked for a miracle. The next day Henry lifted Johnny out of the bed to get him ready for the appointment with Dr. Nather. Manuelita washed him up and clothed him. Then Henry lifted him in his arms and carried him to the car. It was a sight to see Henry carrying his 19 year old son. Johnny looked lifeless as he barely could grasp his dad around his neck.

"Lala, we want you to go with us, your English is better than ours and you can help us understand what the doctor is saying, if we don't understand," said a very down trodden Henry.

They were off to Fort Collins in hope that Dr. Nather could perform a miracle. As they traveled on the road to Fort Collins people would shout out," our prayers are with you Johnny, stay strong."

With a Rosary in her hand, Manuelita gently rolled the beads across her fingers and stayed faithful that the La Virgen would ask Jesus for a blessing and healing. Her face showed signs of grief, but there was a glimpse of hope as she continued with her, 'Santa Marias' and 'Padre Nuestros.' In the back seat Lala also held her Rosary in her left hand and held her big brother with her right arm. As they got closer to the Chiropractor's office their prayers got louder and louder.

Dr. Nather's office was his home. There was nothing similar to a medical office, just a plain old house with a picket fence, a lawn and a statue of the Blessed Virgin in the front yard.

"Welcome to my office, said Dr. Nather as Henry carried Johnny into the office. "Bring him in here and I'll examine him."

This examination was different than that of a regular medical doctor. All of the family was allowed to go into the examination room.

"Now Johnny I need you to lie flat on your back and breathe in and out slowly," said a gentle Dr. Nather. "Now cough!"

Johnny started coughing unceasingly, as the professional laid hands all over his body. He then stopped and pin pointed an area that was in the center of his stomach, right below the diaphragm.

"Now Johnny this is going to hurt, so hang on to his hands, mom and dad," instructed the doc as he massaged the area with great pressure. Then Johnny started vomiting pus and bile from his mouth and then he let out a scream that was so eerie that Lala started crying. The smell was so pungent that it could tear paint off the wall. Lala couldn't stand the smell so she left the room and went outside to get fresh air.

"Don't worry the infection is leaving his body," assured the doctor as he continue to press on Johnny's abdomen. Then the doctor gave Johnny some concoction to drink, a drink with Chinese herbs of some sort.

"Don't worry Johnny this drink will settle your stomach and the healing process will begin. It looks like you had an old injury that never healed and it settled in your abdomen," said the healer.

"Okay Mr. and Mrs. Chacon your son is in the healing process, just give him two ounces of this elixir of Chinese herbs once a day and see me in one week.

Henry, Manuelita and Lala were in shock, they couldn't believe their eyes. Johnny got up from the examination table and walked over to the doctor as if he were never sick and gave him a big hug.

"Thanks doc, I owe my life to you and may God bless and keep you," said a grateful Johnny as he put on his shirt and pants. Johnny then walked to the car and in amazement and Manuelita held her Rosary up to the sky and said, "Gracias Adios."

Lala just stared at her brother in astonishment and couldn't believe her eyes. Her brother was whole again and on the way home he said, "Dad can you stop and buy me a big thick steak, I'm starving to death."

They knew that he was just kidding, like always. It seemed like God still had plans for Johnny.

"Mom do you remember when that garage door fell on me and you just wrapped it up and said that I was going to be okay, and you said that saying, "*sana sana colita de rana*, (heal, heal the tail of a rat," "well that was the injury that the Dr. Nather was talking about," said Johnny as they pulled into the front of the farm home.

"I'm sure glad that Dr. Nather didn't know that saying," said Johnny.

Johnny stepped out of the car into the house. Verlin, Eddie and Rosie couldn't believe their eyes. Their brother was lifeless and now he's walking, talking and home again and ready to take on the world with his jokes and music. From that point on the Chacons would visit Dr. Nather every once in awhile. It didn't matter for what, a cough, a fever, rash, it didn't matter because they had confidence that God directed them to this healer.

Chapter 21

New Mexico Meets Colorado

1941 was a pretty memorable time for the Chacons. Gene and Maggie were engaged to be married. Johnny started to date a young lady named Ermilinda, who went by the name of Billie for short. Grandpa Juan Chacon passed away in the summer and Rose Chacon was 18 and in love.

It so happened, that Rosie met a young gentleman from Variadero, New Mexico. Variadero is a small ranching village in eastern New Mexico, approximately 56 miles east of Las Vegas, New Mexico. His name was Ancelmo Conrado Gonzales. Now because the northern sector of Colorado was in dire need of cheap labor, many '*Manitos,*' Hispanic New Mexicans found themselves working the beet fields. In 1941 there was a big campaign from the big agriculturalists to recruit Hispanos from the San Luis Valley and New Mexico.

Conrado was a hired hand who worked for the Apodacas. He worked directly for Daniel, Lucy's husband. Dan Apodaca was a pretty popular farm worker in the north. He was the prototype, the prime example of a farm worker to all of the farm workers of the north. I guess you can say a farm worker of farm workers. By 1941 Lucy and Daniel had four children. She stayed home while Dan directed many men and families to pick crops and top beets. Conrado proved to be one of the better workers for Dan. His hard work ranching skills were apparent as he breezed through the fields like a gazelle moving and picking without making a sound. But, Rosie caught his eye one day as he topped beets in the next row beside her. She was persistent and worked so fast that Conrado couldn't keep up with her. At the end of each row she'd look back and let out a quiet laugh while he was exhausted from trying to catch her.

"What's wrong 'Manito' can't keep up with the real workers from Colorado?" asked a teasing Rosie as she wiped her brow with her kerchief.

"All you Manitos from New Mexico talk a lot of crap, you are as slow as a turtle," said Rosie as she took a swig of water. My sister Lala can whip you and she's just a fair worker at 14 years old and look my little sister Verlin is 12 and right on your tail."

"Rose you're at the right pace, I love to see you from the back, it's a better view, I love to see you move," said a joking Conrado as he started laughing hysterically.

Well it was a matter of weeks before Conrado finally asked her out to attend a harvest dance. Before you know it Conrado asked for her hand in marriage.

At the end the harvest Conrado was asking Henry if he could take Rose with him to Variadero to introduce her to his parents and family.

Now on the way to Variadero from Las Vegas Conrado's car got a flat tire. It so happened that two young men from Variadero came to the rescue, Liberato and Elijio Quintana. Now these two men were very valiant in their approach. Elijio caught an eye on Lala and wouldn't stop staring at her. Lala was somewhat embarrassed. Conrado told the two men to show a little respect to these two young ladies, because they were too young. After the tire was fixed Conrado went to the Gonzales ranch and introduced his fiancée to his family.

Variadero was somewhat like a desert, very dry and dusty. There wasn't too much work, except for ranching. In order to have a successful ranch business one would have to have thousands of acres to raise cattle, like the Quintanas.

"You know those two young guys that helped us with our tire, well they have a great ranching business with thousands of acres of land and many of cattle," said Conrado as he pointed across the horizon.

"Who'd ever marry those guys would be set for life."

It was Saturday night and there was a dance at Trementina a smaller village near Variadero. All the villagers were there. All of the Ladies sat on one side of the room and all the vaqueros sat on the other side. Juan Quintana was there with his ten gallon hat talking about the ranching business with his compadres. The music was very traditional, a guitar, violin and an accordion was the entertainment. Traditional music from New Mexico was the genre and a mixture of square dance, folk dance, and rancheras were danced.

Elijio couldn't keep his eye off of Lala. So finally he asked her to dance. Lala never really thought anything about it. And that's all it was, a dance. Verlin was very popular with the younger vaqueros and danced all night.

Yes, indeed, this was a very important night for Conrado as he showed off his raving beauty. He was on top of the world whispering sweet nothings in Rosie's ear and danced until his feet were blistered. It didn't matter, he was in love and he wanted to tell the world.

Chapter 22

World War II

The attack of Pearl Harbor on December 7th 1941 marked the date that was the deciding factor which involved the United States in World War II. Pearl Harbor held both American naval and air bases in the Hawaiian Islands. This surprise attack marked the most terrible military disaster in American history. Before this attack, the United States held a position of neutrality. The U.S. never wanted to get involved with the war, but because of the bloodshed on American soil, the U.S. declared war on Japan the next day December 8th 1941. On that date the U.S. joined the allied powers on a global conflict that pitted the world powers against each other. The world was divided into two factions, the Axis powers and the Allied Powers. Germany, Italy and Japan were a part of the Axis Powers. The United States joined the forces of the Allied powers with Great Britain, France and other smaller democratic nations in Europe.

When the people of the United States heard about this attack on American soil they became outraged. Jingoism was the belief that the Americans would avenge the deaths of all the innocent people at Pearl Harbor. Young men throughout the U.S. stormed the recruit offices to join the service to fight against the Axis. Northern Colorado was no different. Every Tom, Dick and Jose joined the ranks.

Gene too caught 'gun ho' fever and didn't want to be left out of the action. So in 1942, Gene joined the Army and became an aviator mechanic and received all of his basic training in the Fiji Islands. Now, there was this thing with Maggie. What was he going to do with Maggie? Well they didn't want to get married until she got out of high school, so she made a vow to wait for her soldier boy.

After basic training Gene found himself stationed in the Philippines, Manila to be exact. The strategy of the United States was that the United States was to set up naval and air bases throughout the Pacific Ocean close in proximity to Japan.

Back on the home front Rose and Conrad became Mr. and Mrs. Conrado Gonzales. They were married in Windsor and the best way to explain it was that it was a great celebration, but Mother Nature wasn't invited, but she sent her R.S.V. P., any way. That night there happened to be a terrible snow storm which stranded everyone at the Westerdahl farm where the reception and dance took place. Just imagine!

So Conrado and Rosie didn't have a honey moon. Days later Rosie and Conrado were on their way back to New Mexico to live on the ranch. It was a sad time for the family to see them leave. Lala and Verlin were the saddest when their older sister left.

"Sister we are going to miss you," said Verlin with a tear in her eye.

" Don't worry my little sister we'll try to come back every three months to visit and who knows if the ranching business doesn't work out we'll be back and find work on one of these farms," said a consoling Rosie as she wiped the tears from Verlin's face.

"Big sister, I'm really going to miss you too, I wish you well and I love you", said Lala as her lower lip shook.

As Henry and Manuelita gave their good byes, Conrado stood by the loaded down car and assured them that everything would be just fine. He made a promise to guard his new wife with his life. Rosie gave her last hugs to Eddie and Johnny and off they were to New Mexico.

Over seas the war became intense. The Axis power under the authority of Adolf Hitler was on a path of destruction. Many innocent people died. In Europe over six million Jews were executed and in the Pacific, Hirohito had control of all in his way.

Where was Gene in all this mess? He was at Legatee Air Force base in the Philippines near Manila. He was part of a crew who repaired planes, built runways and landing fields.

The ranching business was not as lucrative as Conrado expected it to be. The winter was a harsh one. Many of his cattle died and the next spring and summer were so dry that they couldn't fatten their cattle enough for market. Shortly after, Conrado and Rosie found themselves back in

Windsor at the Westerdahl Farm. Rosie has some news to tell her younger sisters.

"You know its sure nice being back home with my family," said content Rosie Gonzales. "It sure was boring on the ranch, nothing to do, a complete boredom."

Then she called her two younger sisters Lala and Verlin over to the bedroom and said, "Feel my stomach."

Lala and Verlin apprehensively touched her stomach.

Verlin said," Why is it moving, like you're hungry?"

Rosie just sat there laughing out of control, holding her side and crying at the same time.

"No silly there's a real baby inside of me. I'm going to have a baby."

Verlin and Lala continued to touch Rosie's stomach and cried with joy as they felt the baby move in Rosie's stomach. Then the two sisters looked at each other in total amazement.

"You see that's life growing inside of me. It's a miracle from God," explained Rosie. "You are going to be aunties," said a proud Rosie as she turned to give her sisters a hug. "This is obviously not the first time, with big sister Lucy having four children Beatrice, Alfredo, Manuel and Margaret."

Six months later, Rosie gave birth to little Isabelle Gonzales.

The Chacons were so happy with the new addition. But to survive on the farm during this time was very hard, especially with more mouths to feed.

Johnny and Conrado had to relocate because they had landed a job at the steel mill in Pueblo, so they moved to Pueblo for short while. The longevity of their job was very short, for they were there for a few months and then they were laid off.

The only recourse for Conrado was the Army. Uncle Sam was calling him to go to the south Pacific to fight against the Japanese and Hirohito.

The Philippine Islands were so beautiful. So green and lush were its jungles and the best sandy beaches. The mountains were full of greenery. The people were so friendly and inviting. The people spoke Tagalog and Ilocano. Tagalog was a language spoken that had some qualities of Spanish and the native dialect. So when Gene arrived in Manila he would hear parts of his native Spanish in their dialog and conversation. It's too bad that such beautiful islands and people had to be part of such a brutal war.

Tokyo Rose was driving the U.S. military crazy with her announcements over the radio. She was a Japanese refugee who escaped from the California internment camps and set up a defense against the U.S by making false announcements of where the Japanese Kamikazes would attack next, but sometimes her announcements were true. So like a false alarm at a school, the firemen still have to prepare and investigate. The U.S feared Tokyo Rose so every precaution was taken.

One day during lunch, Tokyo Rose made an announcement over the radio waves stating that Legatee was going to be bombed. She even said the time and exact venue, the mess hall. As soon as they heard her announcement the entire mess hall was evacuated, five minutes later the mess hall was more than a mess, it was a giant crater on the ground.

Quickly the U.S. deployed all of their troops from all of the bases in the Pacific. The U.S. was on a mission to destroy the Japanese. From the Philippines and other bases throughout the Pacific, the Ocean was filled with ships as far as the eye could see. It looked like the ancient days of Troy where Achilles was in pursuit of Hermes in the Mediterranean Sea to control all of Greece. Yes, the U.S. was on a mission. These surprise attacks had to stop!

Chapter 23

Dear Gene

After six months of the U.S. firebombing many small Japanese cities, President Harry S. Truman ordered the Japanese cities of Hiroshima and Nagasaki to be bombed using the atomic bomb. Hiroshima was the first to be bombed on August 6th 1945. While Nagasaki was bombed on August 9th 1945. On August 15th Japan surrendered to the Allied powers.

Ironically enough, through happenstance, Conrado did spend some time with Gene in the Philippines, to be exact in 1943 at Luzon. But Conrado also was deployed to fight off the attacks of the Japanese.

Back home in Windsor, Henry and Manuelita were very worried about their son and son in-law. During this time their prayers were strong. Henry even met with a group of Penitentes in Wattenberg. They would pray and sing the alabados of the days in Trinidad.

Periodically, Gene received letters from his fiancée Maggie Moore to discuss and plan their marriage. But while Gene was off in the Pacific protecting our freedoms, Maggie met up with a sergeant who was on military leave and married him. When Gene received his "Dear John" letter, he was devastated. He was quite in love with her and her deception really hurt him.

When he returned back home his parents heard about her dishonesty. They too felt Gene's pain. Manuelita wanted to say, "I told you so," but kept it to herself in respect of her son's feelings.

One Saturday afternoon brother-in-law Dan Apodaca and Gene decided to go to the local bar in Windsor to have a couple of beers. Gene was dressed in his military suit and was so proud that he was an American citizen. When they arrived at the bar Dan immediately went to the rear of the bar out in back where the outside patio was.

"Dan, where are you going?" asked Gene as he followed Dan to the bar.

"Don't you know Gene that we cannot sit in the main part of the bar," said a hesitant Dan. "We are required to sit in the back patio, see the sign. "NO MEXICANS ALLOWED!"

"That's a bunch of bull shit!" cursed Gene as he walked into the main entrance. "Don't they know that I' m a decorated soldier who fought against the Japanese and Germans for their freedoms! BULL SHIT"

Dan stayed in the back patio while Gene sat down and ordered a beer. Everyone kept staring at Gene. No one said a word to him. Then one of the patrons walked to the bar and said, "What is this beaner doing in this bar, doesn't he know about the rule of 'separate but equal.' Make him sit in the patio with all of the other MEXICANS!"

The owner of the bar knew Gene previously from involvement in the local Catholic Church. "Gene you have to sit in the back patio with all of the other Mexican Americans, it's a rule of this bar. "I don't want to call the cops, so go to the back or leave."

Gene sat there for a few seconds and said, "See this uniform, it represents the United States. While overseas I risked my life for all ethnics groups and races, and now I can't order a beer like a decent human being? You are treating me like an illegal alien! That's a bunch of BULL SHIT! BULL SHIT! You can stick the beer up your ASS!"

You see even after the war Americans with Spanish surnames still had to be separated. Jim Crow laws were still honored after WWII and the government did nothing about it. Gene was so embarrassed by this incident all he could do was curse the owner out. Yes, it was quite the embarrassment. These people not only fed our country but they also served in the military to protect our freedoms. Gene was ridiculed by this incident; people today would not condone such racism and discrimination. Because Gene broke the rule of the bar he was looked at as trouble maker. This act of discrimination was so accepted it became a social institution. It was not until the Civil Rights Movement of the 1960's that these obvious acts of discrimination were brought to court and were proven to be unconstitutional.

When Gene came back from the war he found Henry, Manuelita and the children all living in a little shack outside of Windsor. When he saw this, his heart was broken to see his parents living in such poverty. Because he had just left the service he had saved enough money to bring his parents to a home in Denver, plus the G.I. Bill would also help them attain a home. Johnny was now married to Ermilinda also known as Billie, and had two daughters who lived in Fort Collins. He was working in the mountains in a new mountain town called Granby. A new addition had been added to the family, Judy Joann Duran who became a Chacon because Manuelita's sister, Ramona was committed to a mental institution. Ramona gave birth to little Joann in the institution. Her dad couldn't raise her. So she became a Chacon at the age of two months. At age 5 Joann's disabilities had become apparent. So in addition to the Chacon's poverty they raised a baby with a mental disability. But, oh how they loved her.

Henry explained to Gene that while he was off to war, the U.S. had contracted with Mexico to bring in workers to fill the void of all the men going to war. In short there was a need for labor in the fields. The program was called the Bracero program. These people worked for less money than the native Hispanos so in essence the Hispanos who were the true Americans had no jobs, no source of income. This was the time to make another move, Denver.

When times got tough good old dependable migration was available. The move, the transition, the exodus, the immigration, the journey were all at the finger tips of the migrant, when in doubt move. It sounds simple but through all of the transition there was always a lot of pain and tribulation.

Chapter 24

Back to Denver

His name was Eugenio; he would be the one to carry the name onto the next generations, born July 13th 1917. On that momentous day Henry and Manuelita declared Eugenio a genius, having great hope that this little one would one day take them out of poverty.

When Henry dedicated his son to the Lord on July 13th 1917, he knew that Gene would be the one to take his family out of that vicious cycle of poverty and migration. Gene's parents were so proud of their son. He came back alive from World War II and had represented the family with such honor. World War II had taken so many lives, but Gene survived. It was a blessing from God. All of those Rosaries said had come to fruition and now it was like new to know that there was hope.

When the Chacons first came to Denver, Gene landed a job with Swift Packing House, Henry got a job at Gates Rubber Company. Lala and Verlin were hired at Cascade Laundry. Manuelita stayed home took care of Joann and the rest of the children were starting their own families. Lucy was in Windsor. Rosie was in Brighton. Eddie was in Denver, also with his parents and Johnny was raising his two girls in Fort Collins.

Their new residence was 27th and Larimer on the east side of Denver across from historic Sacred Heart Catholic Church. Again the new residence was in a neighborhood with many Hispanos. They felt comfortable living in a place where they felt welcomed. The people were like them. They were all 'gente' their people of color. They spoke a mixed dialect called Spanglish, a combination of English and Spanish. At a whim they could switch from one language to the next and fluently. It was quite an experience to listen to the fluidity of this language. Sometimes the words were said incorrectly or out of context, but yet everyone knew what they were saying.

Living on the east side of Denver in 1947 was quite different than living in the rural farmland of northern Colorado. Jobs were plentiful in Denver, post-World War II. The field work was now being done by all of the Mejicanos who stayed back after the war during the Bracero Program. The Mejicanos too loved the United States and saw it as a land of opportunity. So many Mejicanos stayed at all costs. Because of their stay, the Native Hispano at a great influx migrated to the big city to make an honest living.

City life was at a faster pace than the farm life. Many people had their own transportation and if you had no vehicle to get around there was the city bus or trolley car. Henry would take the city bus to south Denver where Gates Rubber Company was located. Cascade Laundry was in walking distance from the Chacon's apartment on Larimer Street. Swift Meat Packing was located on the northern side of Denver called Globeville. Washington Street held more than one packing meat company. There also was Capital, United and Cudahy's.

A special culture had developed. Because of the incorporation of the union a unique lifestyle took place. The packing house was your typical factory. There were people working there from all ethnic and racial backgrounds. They were the working class of America.

Gene and Eddie were making lots of money at the packing house and before you knew it Gene had enough money for a down payment on a duplex. Well this made sense, a duplex where his parents and sisters could live on one side and Eddie and Gene on the other side. So again the Chacons moved to 35th and Marion. The new owners were so happy and it was all a blessing from God.

While everyone was off to work Manuelita was at home occupied with Joanne. Joanne would run Manuelita ragged. When the grandchildren came over to visit, Joanne loved to pinch them. Grandma Manuelita would be so apologetic that she got tired of saying, "I'm sorry, she doesn't know any better. Please don't get mad at her."

Manuelita was so exhausted at the end of the day that when Verlin and Lala got home from working at the laundry, they would have to relieve her from her hard day with Joanne. They constantly had to keep their eyes on her, because Joanne would always find herself in the most precarious situations.

Lala and Verlin loved the laundry. The work was hard but nothing like the fields. The only similarity to the fields was the extreme heat from the steam irons. Sometimes it would get up to 100 degrees plus. But it was a job and it was bringing in the money.

The environment of the laundry was very jovial, everyone got along well. Yes you had your typical cliques and disagreements, but generally speaking it was a very productive business.

During lunch one day Lala and Verlin ate lunch with Shirley Rodriguez. She was telling them that her sister was looking for a good clean cut man, in other words her sister was looking for a husband.

"Say Lala do you happen to know any good clean cut men that my sister could meet and possibly be available for marriage?" asked an inquisitive Shirley as she took a long puff from her cigarette. "My sister is looking and all that is out there is a bunch of vagabonds."

"We have an older brother who is available," said Verlin. "He just came out of the service and has a real good job at Swift Meat Packing. He owns our house and he's really smart!"

"When can we set up this meeting?" asked Shirley as she swallowed her last bites of lunch. "Why not this weekend? It will be great, we'll go over for lunch and I'll bring Esther over and you guys supply the rest."

All during the week the girls talked about this match made in heaven. They talked about preparing a special meal and what Esther should wear. Esther wasn't too sure about this meeting at the Chacons. Verlin was prepared and brought a photo Gene when he was in the Army.

"Shirley, show this photo to Esther and let us know what she thinks, if this all works out maybe we'll go into the match making business. We can be certified match makers," laughed Lala as she showed the photo to Shirley.

"This is your brother, he sure is a babe! Maybe you can set me up with him," joked Shirley as she gawked at the photo of Gene. Just kidding, I'll show Esther the photo of this movie star. She'll be pleased."

"We'll tell Gene about this meeting at lunch on Saturday," said Lala as they left work and walked across the street.

That evening the girls confronted Gene and asked him if he would like to meet a young lady who was interested in him. Gene tried to give his sisters this image of, "oh I'm so strict and you better respect your elders."

So he was sometimes hard to talk to, remember he was 10 years older than the girls.

"Oh, it's not going to hurt just to meet this Erma," said a serious Eugenio.

"Gene, her name is Esther, Esther, so don't be calling her Erma!" exclaimed Verlin.

"Just kidding, said Gene, I'll be a gentleman."

That Saturday came quickly. It was 12 noon on Saturday and a person could cut the anticipation with a knife. Verlin and Lala were preparing a nice lunch for Esther and Gene when a knock came at the door.

"That must be Esther and Shirley. I sure hope that they hit it off. It sure would be nice if Gene would find himself a woman, he needs a woman badly to give him direction in life. We also need someone to carry on the Chacon name," said Lala.

Then Eddie walked into the room and said, "What do I look like, chop liver, my son will carry on the name of the Chacons. Girls, don't you forget it!"

"Okay Romeo, we need to see some evidence before you spout off," said Verlin. You need to find a woman first! Then we'll believe you."

Gene was very cordial when he met Esther. But Esther played the hard to get role. Gene was persistent in his approach and in days they were dating and it was official! Immediately he was attracted to her. He was attracted to her and proposed and married Esther Rodriguez on February 28th 1948.

So the duplex was now inhabited by Gene and his new bride Mrs. Eugenio Chacon. They lived on one side and the rest of the family lived on the other side. It was quite crowded and in a couple of years it was time for the main family to move out and get a new abode so they could be comfortable. The next move was on the east side at 33rd avenue.

Chapter 25

At a Young Age

...Then number three followed on June 24ᵗʰ 1920 with Juan Bautista Chacon, Henry Christened him a musician and entertainer...

When I think of Johnny Chacon I like to compare him to a JFK or a Martin Luther King but of course on a smaller scale. Johnny was prominent in the Chacon Family. He was funny and boy could he could he entertain with his guitar! Well, at least what Mom has told me about him. You see Johnny and Lala had a special connection, probably because of their great music ability. He was inspirational. His jokes were comical and he was very tenacious when it came to never giving up, as proven when he almost died at a very young age and overcoming death when doctors thought he had Tuberculosis.

Charismatic would probably be the best word to describe him. When he walked into a room people would know that there was something special about him. When he talked everyone would listen, because they knew that something hysterical was about to happen. He was considered to be the focal point of the family and when the cousins came over they all wanted to know where Johnny was. He was just a cool guy.

In 1948 while the majority of the Henry Chacon family were living in Denver. Johnny Chacon and his family lived in la colonia in Fort Collins. His lovely wife was Ermilinda, known as Billie. They had two daughters Helen and Beatrice. He was a construction worker and was responsible for working on the construction of bridges in Granby, a new town being developed in the mountains.   Granby was quite the distance from Fort Collins, so occasionally Johnny would car pool to work daily. But one day he made the decision to go home after a hard day's work in bad weather conditions. The roads were not in the best condition and in bad weather could be very treacherous.

So one day Johnny set off from Fort Collins with his two coworkers Joe Madrid and Don Martinez. It took about two hours to get to Granby from Fort Collins. The routine of the day was quite laborious and task filled. The crew did a lot of heavy lifting, driving of heavy equipment like front end loaders, dump trucks, cherry pickers and earth movers. Johnny's expertise in handling heavy duty equipment came when he worked at Red Feathers in the C.C. camps.

"Johnny they're predicting a big rain storm about the time we're leaving this evening," said Joe Madrid as he pointed to the northern sky. "Maybe the big honcho could let us out a little early so we can make it home safely."

As the day progressed the sky was filled with clouds. Every second it became darker and a slight wind was coming from the north. In about an hour the temperature dropped 30 degrees. Then rains came down slowly in sprinkles and then in big drops and before you know it was torrential.

"Johnny, it's raining buckets out here, maybe we should stay overnight at the lodge and go home after work tomorrow," shouted Don Martinez as he tried to talk over the thunder and loud wind.

"Don't be such a sissy, boys we'll make it home in time for our lady's great cooking, chili verde sounds good about now," shouted Johnny as he jumped into the car.

The boys waited about 5 minutes and then they were off down the mountain to Fort Collins. Johnny had a hard time seeing the road. So Joe opened the passenger window to help Johnny get a better view of the road.

"Pull over John! Safety is an issue here! So pull over!" said a frantic Don.

Within minutes they came up on a vehicle that was moving very slowly. Johnny wanted to pass on the left side but the driver in the car stayed in the middle of the lane and wouldn't let Johnny pass. Then the rain ceased and the sun started to shine barely as it became sunset. The couple was persistent to stay in the middle of the lane.

"What's wrong with these people, are they deaf? Can't they hear my horn?" asked an impatient Johnny as he pulled his car alongside the other vehicle.

When he pulled left alongside the other car he saw an elderly couple just using every precaution necessary in driving in the mountains. When Johnny made eye contact with the other driver he signaled to them so that they would pull over. When he looked up he found no lane to drive and then lost total control of the vehicle. With no lane to drive on he drove off the side of the mountain. They were like laundry inside a dryer, tumbling, tumbling all the way to the bottom of the mountain.

When Don and Joe woke up they found themselves inside Kremlin Hospital. They had superficial wounds, scratches and bruises. Johnny was pronounced dead when he arrived at the hospital. Later his wife was asked to identify her husband.

The wound in Manuelita's heart was huge. Someone once said, "One should never have to bury their own child." No one knows the pain a mother bares for own children. Johnny's siblings were devastated from their brother's death. No one can fill the void of a very special person like Johnny Bautista Chacon, a humorist, singer, guitarist, a father, husband, a great friend and my Uncle!

From the stories Mom told me about Uncle Johnny, it was like I knew him. His spirit lives with all of his nieces and nephews and many of us have carried on the music and laughter of Johnny Chacon, the Entertainer...

Chapter 26

Like a Movie Star...

As a young boy I'd see Mom's youngest sister Verlin and she just reminded me of movie star. She was such a beautiful woman. When Auntie Verlin and Mom sang duets they were like two angels singing so beautifully. She is always so loving and caring and when you see her it's always a kiss on the cheek and you are sure getting handsome.

It sure seems as if Cascade Laundry was a place for match making. First Gene finds his soul mate in Esther and now it's Verlin who finds her knight in shining armor.

After Johnny's death, Verlin was very sad. She grieved for months and at times would get very sick. She missed a lot of days of work at Cascade but one day her loss was filled with a special guy who caught her eye.

"Hey Rodrigo, what do you think about those two babes that Cascade just hired?" asked Paul as he emptied the clothes bin.

"Which two babes, there are a lot of babes here,' responded Rodrigo as he pointed at the main floor of the laundromat.

"Come on Rodrigo, now your pulling my leg, you know who I'm talking about," said Paul. "Those two there, working on the steam presses."

"Which one do you like?" asked Rodrigo.

"I'm favoring the cute one with the mole on her face, said Paul. "But the other one is pretty also."

"She sure is pretty," said Rodrigo.

Several days had passed and each day Paul would find ways to go down to visit the main floor of the laundromat. Each time Paul would go down to the main floor he'd tried to make eye contact with Verlin. She was quite the lady at first and wouldn't give him the time of the day. But eventually he was able to get a smile from her.

"Rodrigo, I'm making some progress, she actually smiled at me, boy! She sure is beautiful," said an excited Paul.

"Paul, you should ask her out on a date," said Rodrigo

"Come on Rodrigo, you know that I'm too shy to ask the most beautiful woman in the world for a date," responded Paul.

"Here's the plan Paul, you write her a love note and I'll take it down to her, is that good or not?" asked Paul reluctantly.

During the last break of the day Rodrigo and Paul conjured up a love note to send to Verlin. He asked her out and needed her to write back a response and give the note to Rodrigo after work.

After work Rodrigo received the note and Verlin said that she was willing to meet Paul after work to have coffee with him. The moment was intense to say the least. Paul waited for Verlin and introduced himself and what was so funny he was stuttering and shaking like a leaf. Verlin thought that was cute and accepted his invitation to have a formal date.

Paul and Verlin hit it off pretty good. They dated for awhile and fell deeply in love and on April 12th 1949 they became Mr. and Mrs. Paul Salazar.

Chapter 27

The Denver Academy, a Conflict of Standards

Days had passed since Verlin's departure of the Chacon family. Lala was lost without her baby sister. So she started to hang out with her niece Beatrice Apodaca, who had been studying in Denver to be a stenographer. It wasn't too long after Verlin left the Chacon abode that Mary and Beatrice went dancing at the Denver Academy. It happened to be New Year's Eve and the Ladies were open to some good old fashion clean cut fun.

Now for sure that's one thing that Mary was a connoisseur of, music. She loved to dance and sing. She knew every top 40 song of the day and when it came to dancing she knew the latest step, may it be the swing, jitterbug, waltz or the two-step.

The Denver Academy was located on the east side of Denver and was famous for its great dances and fun entertainment. Its clientele were primarily servicemen from all military branches. Most of these men were stationed at Fitzsimmons and Lowry Air Force Base.

When Lala and Beatrice walked into the hall every soldier did a double take. They could not keep their eyes off the young ladies. From the time they walked in, to the time it was closed, Beatrice and Lala were dancing like there was no tomorrow. Men were lining up to dance with them. They were having so much fun. Lala really enjoyed dancing with everyone but there was one special guy that repeatedly kept asking her out to dance. His name was Mitch Mitchell.

Mitch was a very good looking guy he stood 5'9" and had the bluest eyes, blonde and was very muscular. He was from the south side of Denver and just completed his term in the Army.

After the dance he wanted Lala's phone number and to know, when they could meet again. She told him to call in a couple of days. Then momentarily, Eddie drove up.

"So who's the gabacho?" asked Eddie.

"Oh! None of your business, just someone I just met, who's really a great dancer and such a nice guy," declared Lala as she climbed into the car.

"I always thought that you wouldn't go out with a 'white guy,' since all of that discrimination we experienced in Weld County and all of those fights you had with those guys in school," reminded Eddie as he turned the car into the drive way of their home.

"Well he seemed to be a pretty nice guy, I can't judge them all alike," argued Lala. There are good and bad in all races."

"Go to bed Eddie, you're just jealous!" exclaimed Lala as she went into her mother's bedroom to tell her she was safely home.

All night long Mary thought about the guy she just met. "Will he call me, like he said he would? Or will he be a jerk like all of the guys I've met in the past. I guess time will tell. I'll give him a couple of days and that's it!" Thought, Lala... "That's it!"

That night Lala fell into a deep sleep and found herself in a big leafy green field. She lay in the field on her back and could see rainbows above. The sky was cloudy with whirl winds in the east. Then the rain came down in buckets. In seconds the rain stopped and the sky was filled with a beautiful blue. In the west you could see a man in the distant carrying a huge brown gunny sack. When the man got within speaking distance he said, "how do you do my name is M.M. and I love to purchase and sell, kind of like a peddler.

"I see that you are enamored."

"How can you tell that I'm enamored?" asked Lala.

"I can tell by the green mole on your face. Here on this island if you have a green mole on your face that means that you're falling in love," said the man with the gunny sack.

"That's impossible, I've only met one guy in the past day or so and I'm in love? That's preposterous!" said Lala as she tried to look into the gunny sack.

"What's in the bag, M.M?" asked Lala.

"Oh, a special herb with adventure in its future," replied M.M.

"What do you do with this herb?" asked Lala

"You drink it with a big glass of water and then the sweetest dreams come about. Then you choose one of the dreams to live and that's your life," foretold M.M.

"Would you love to try some?" asked M.M.

"Oh no," responded Lala, "I've never taken drugs before."

"Come on Lala, you choose the dream that's going to give you the most adventure in your life. Come on live a little," coaxed M.M.

"Okay M.M. I'll try it if it gets you off my back, said Lala hesitantly.

So Lala grabbed a big handful of the herb from the gunny sack stuffed it in her mouth, chewed it and drank it down with a big glass of water. Slowly the herb was working, and then the dreams came like crazy. She had many dreams. She had dreams about failure, success, past events; like the passing of her grandfathers and brother, working in the fields and winning all of those singing competitions. But the most prolific dream was a reoccurring dream about going to Las Vegas and becoming very rich. It so happened in the dream that M.M. became her husband and they would sell this special herb to people to help them get rich in Vegas. The good part of all of this is that it made them rich also, filthy rich. So she chose the dream about getting rich in Vegas.

The lifestyle of Vegas was very demanding for Ms. Lala and Mr. M.M. Many people became addicted to this herb in Vegas so the supply of the herb was growing scarce. Engagements were being broken daily. The dream of Vegas was dying slowly and an inner voice was telling Lala that she chose the wrong dream. The big gunny sack was no longer big, but getting smaller each day. Then mysteriously M.M. was nowhere to be found. He was lost in a lost dream. Where could he be? Lala searched high and low but she could not find her supplier. You see the herb gave her this life, but M.M. forgot to tell her to sustain this livelihood she would have to take this herb for the rest of her life. Las Vegas now became a true desert for her as she longed to be with her parents on the east side of Denver.

The next morning Lala woke up and could not believe the dream that she had. What does this dream mean? Was there symbolization which will give me a clue? Oh well, maybe my prayers have to be stronger and more consistent. Like Mom always says, La Virgen will give me the answer.

A couple of days had passed and sure enough Mary received her phone call.

"Hello, may I speak to Lala Chacon?" asked Mitch.

"Wait a second," responded Henry, "Lala, you're wanted on the phone."

So the conversation continued and they talked about how much fun they had at the Denver Academy. They had so much fun that they agreed to see each other again. For six months Mitch and Lala went dancing on weekends and frequent the movie theatres. It was official they were going steady.

Mitch had just finished his term with the Army six months earlier and was still trying to find employment. He was well mannered and showed the utmost respect to Lala and her family. Would this man from the south side who rode a bus to the Chacons every weekend be Lala's destiny?

Manuelita and Henry really liked Mitch. Henry even offered to try to get him a job at Gates. Henry and Manuelita were open when it came to Lala dating Mitch who was not of Hispanic descent. Lala was the first in the family to date an Anglo. Henry and Manuelita had many bad experiences with discrimination in Weld County, but Mitch was different as he was very respectful and tolerant of people's differences.

Like I said earlier, Mitch was unemployed and was searching for great opportunity to take Lala away from a struggling life and make her a queen. So one day Mitch came over with great news. He wanted Lala to go outside when she went outside Mitch said, "I want to take you away from all of this and take you to a place where we can make tons of money. Look Lala, I just bought this 1949 Ford coup and I'm ready to take you to Nevada where we can make the loot."

Mary just stood there in astonishment. She could not believe what she had just heard... "How are we going to make a living in Nevada?" asked Lala. "We don't have jobs!"

At that moment Mitch opened the trunk of his coup and lo and behold there it was a big brown gunny sack filled with marijuana, neatly put in little plastic bags.

"Lala, this is how we are going to be rich in Las Vegas, Nevada," responded Mitch. "We'll sell the dope to the gangsters in Vegas and get rich, come on Lala come with me, please."

Then a man who was sitting in the front seat came out of the car and said, "M.M.! We need to get out of here, give your lady a kiss and let's get down to business."

"Okay Lala, give me your answer tonight, I'll give you a call and let your parents know that I plan on marrying you in Vegas, said Mitch as he jumped into the driver's seat, "I'll call you tonight."

Mitch waved at her and was on his way. Lala just looked in amazement. "Did he call him M.M.? Of course he did, this is sounding too much like my dream. I'm freaking out!"

That night at supper, Lala discussed the circumstance with her parents. Now Lala was very truthful about Mitch. Henry and Manuelita felt that Mitch was no good and his future could only mean prison.

"Selling drugs can only mean trouble," Lala you deserve better," exclaimed Henry. So when he calls this evening tell him good bye forever."

"Okay Dad, thank you for your advice," said Lala as she wiped the tears from her eyes.

"Did God forewarn me about Mitch through the dream about the dreams and the gunny sack? And of course he let me know that M.M. stood for Mitch Mitchell," thought Lala.

So that evening, Lala gave Mitch Mitchell the bad news and wished him well in his endeavors. He was very disappointed, but said that he'd write her and keep in touch. Lala was cordial and said that maybe one day they would meet again.

Two months later Lala happened to read the news and read that Mitch and his associate were arrested for selling marijuana in Las Vegas. They were convicted and sentenced for ten years in the Nevada State Prison. Lala was relieved that she never went to Las Vegas. Manuelita even cried when she heard that Mitch was in prison for distribution of marijuana and that Lala made the right decision to stay back in Colorado.

Chapter 28

Crossing Paths

Annually, there has been a Labor Day Harvest Carnival in Windsor as far back as who knows when. This harvest carnival culminated the long harvest of all of the crops in the north of Weld and Larimer Counties. It was a time to celebrate and people came from all over to party.

The year was 1950 and Lala was a 23 years old and single. She was the last of the Chacon girls to be married. On Labor Day, Lala invited Beatrice to chum around at the carnival. Beatrice was the eldest daughter of Dan and Lucy Apodaca.

When it came to hanging out with Aunt Lala, Beatrice was so excited. She emulated her. She thought that her aunt was such a great role model. She wished that she had her beautiful shapely body and beautiful sounding voice. But Beatrice was quite the looker herself but, very young at 15. Dan had a sharp, protective eye on his hijita, but, with Aunt Lala they felt very comfortable.

Now, as I said earlier the carnival was one giant party. Featured each year were two dance platforms one for the younger folk and one for the older folk. It so happened that an entourage of young guys came from New Mexico to celebrate the harvest.

Lala and Beatrice were having a ball, dancing on the plat form for the younger adults. When an unexpectedly a young gentleman tapped her on the shoulder and said," Excuse me miss, may I have this dance?"

"Do I know you from somewhere?" asked Lala as she stared at him with bewilderment. She thought to herself, who is this guy? I recognize his funny Spanish accent and that ridiculous Charlie Chaplin looking moustache, but I can't put two and two together."

"It's me Lala, don't you remember? It's Elijio Quintana from Variadero New Mexico, where your brother in law Conrado is from. You can call me Joe for short," said Joe Quintana. This is my nephew Natividad Lucero, but we call him Tive' for short. He is also from the ranch at Variadero."

"What are you doing here in Windsor?" asked Lala.

"I was just visiting my brother Lee in Denver. You met him at the Ranch when we fixed Conrado's flat tire back when..."said Joe as he stared at Lala. I'm here in Windsor to have a good time. In Denver I'm seeking employment and will find out on Monday if I have a job at United Fryar's and Stillman's another packing house."

"Well, do you want to?"

"Want to what?" asked Lala.

"Dance, dance Lala," responded Joe, as he grabbed her by the hand and walked her to the dance platform for the younger crowd.

She never had a chance to respond as he continued to take her to the platform. The first song played was a very popular song of the day, "In the Mood." In the Mood was a jitter bug song, similar to the swing when the girl is swung into the air also with a lot of spins and turns.

Lala loved to dance and apparently Joe was quite the 'Fred Astaire,' old twinkle toes himself. He had some awesome moves for being a vaquero from a ranch in New Mexico.

"Where did you learn to dance so smoothly?" asked Lala as she stopped for a breath of air. Whew, you're tiring me out."

"I learned to dance at a private school at 'El Rito' private school in northern New Mexico. We had dances all the time. I've won many jitterbug contests," boasted a proud Elijio.

"Is Lala short for something?" asked Joe.

"Yes it's short for Candelaria and in school they called me Mary," responded Mary.

"Well, I'll call you Mary from now on," if that's okay.

"Sure," said Mary...

So Joe and Mary laughed and danced until the carnival was over. Tive' and Beatrice were also having fun dancing and walking around the carnival riding the rides and playing the games. Tive was really good at the games and had won several stuffed animals for Beatrice.

At the end of the night Joe and Tive wanted to take Mary and Beatrice for a ride around Windsor. They wanted to cruise Main Street and grab something to eat when Dan, Beatrice's father came around the corner and saw the girls talking to the guys from New Mexico.

"Beatrice it's time to go! Come on say good bye and vamanos!" shouted Dan, "Vamanos!"

So the night was over and Mary and Beatrice had to go home with Dan.

"Joe, I have to go now, maybe one day we'll meet again, I sure had fun, "said Mary as she gave Joe a big hug.

Joe and Tive just stood there disappointed and slowly walked back to their car.

"Those were probably the best two good looking chicks I've ever seen in my life," said Tive as they drove back to Lee's home in Denver.

As Beatrice and Mary walked back to the car, they both talked about how much fun they had. Beatrice thought that Tive was a real sweet guy and Mary couldn't get over how great Joe was at jitterbugging. For when it came to dancing, that's one thing that was Joe's forte.

"How coincidental it was for me to come across Joe again after 9 years," said Mary. "It's just so hard to believe that he's come across my path. He's good looking, kind of short, *peloncito* (balding) and he has the curliest hair. Maybe he's the one."

That monday morning Joe was hired at United Fryar's and Stillman in Globeville. Swift packing house was just down the road. At this time Joe moved in with his nephew Nick Gonzales. Nick at this time had been married for several years to Margaret and had 3 daughters, Diane, Marcella and Josie.

At age 27 Joe was getting pretty restless. He was still a bachelor and was always the third wheel when it came to hanging out with his brother Liberato or his nephew Nick. He too believed that it was time to find him a woman

"Hey Joe when are you going to find yourself a senorita?" asked Margaret. "It's time to go out on your own and quit being such a momma's boy. Do you have a special girl in mind?"

"Well there's this one girl I met in Windsor, her name is Mary Chacon," said Joe.

"Does she have a sister named Rosa?" asked Margaret. "Who's married to Conrado? You know that Conrado is cousin to Nick, your nephew? You know Joe; by coincidence I happen to have Mary's phone number right here."

"Yes, it's the same girl, but she lives in Windsor and I can't go to Windsor, it's too far," said Joe.

"No Joe, she lives here on the east side of Denver on 33rd avenue," said Margaret. "Now that you have a secure job, it's time! Joe it's time! Don't be shy, don't be shy!"

Joe was really excited about Mary living so close to Margaret and Nick on the East side of Denver. Actually Nick and Margaret lived on one side of a duplex and Lee (Joe's brother) and Mary lived on the other side. So everything was in proximity.

"Now all I'll have to do is ask Margaret to ask Mary Chacon if she'll go out with me," thought Joe as he sat down for some lunch.

Several days had passed, and finally Joe got enough guts to ask Margaret to give Mary Chacon a call. So that evening Margaret called Mary and told her that Joe really enjoyed her company at the carnival for Labor Day and wanted to see you again.

Lala was barely over the relationship break up with Mitch when Margaret Gonzales gave her a call asking her if she'd like to go out with Joe. Lala remembered the good time she had with Joe and that he was such a gentleman that night. "He loves to dance and so do I. We'll dance like there's no tomorrow," thought Lala.

So they were off on weekends to the Rainbow ballroom, La Bamba Night Club, the 39th Club, and the Coronado Club to name a few. So again they crossed each other's paths and would go to any and every dance available. Because they lived on the east side near lower down town they found themselves frequently at 23rd and Larimer, at J's Grill. At this joint it seemed as if the north came in contact with the south, in other words where New Mexico came in contact with Colorado. Yes the people that would frequent this bar were either from New Mexico or Northern Colorado. Joe's nephew Bernie Lucero and Lee Quintana played in a band there. Joe also played rhythm on the guitar but preferred to court Mary Chacon. Bernie was the lead guitarist, and Lee played the fiddle.

So the courting ritual continued for several months until one day Margaret and Nick Gonzales met with Henry and Manuelita Chacon and asked them through a letter if Mary would like to be the bride of Joe Quintana. Now as the tradition continued if Henry, Manuelita, and Mary agreed upon Joe Quintana, they would write a letter to Joe accepting the proposal and if the answer was no, a pumpkin would be delivered. Joe's mother was living in New Mexico, so she would not be available for the protocol. So Nick and Margaret served as the surrogate parents of Joe.

Fortunately for Joe, Mary accepted the invitation to be his wife. Upon the acceptance, Joe Quintana became the happiest man alive. On April 29th 1952, they became Mr. and Mrs. Jose Elijio Delacruz Quintana.

Chapter 29

Eddie

Born number five, he was the hardest to be born, but ended up being the best behaved of the Chacon clan...

Eddie was a very good son to Manuelita and Henry. His weekly wages usually went all to his mom for the survival of the family's monthly bills. Since the beginning Manuelita held the money for the household. Henry was too liberal with his earnings, meaning that he liked to spend his hard earned cash on the non-essentials of life, like whisky and chewing tobacco. Manuelita was so conservative that she could squeeze blood from a turnip. Her conservatism was what made the family survive in good and bad times.

Eddie was the last of the children to get married. Several months after Mary and Joe got married; Eddie met a lady who was a distant cousin of Joe's. Her name was Erminda Quintana from Cerritos, New Mexico, one of the first Spanish settlements in New Mexico. Again we see another New Mexico Colorado connection.

Erminda Quintana had followed her Aunt Josefita and Uncle Cleofas Gonzales to Ault, Colorado to work in the beet fields. The beet fields were not for Erminda. She chose to work in a restaurant business in town. So she found a roommate to share the expenses of an apartment in the town. Aunt Josefita and Uncle Cleofas went back to the ranch in New Mexico and she opted to stay in Ault.

She was best described as a very hard worker who labored excessive hours at the local café. With her slender and agile physique she could work all of the other waitresses into the ground. One day, a man who had visited this restaurant on his way to Wyoming noticed her tremendous work ethic, when it came to serving her customers. He was a restaurant entrepreneur in Fort Lupton which was about fifty miles south of Ault. This man offered her twice the pay than the Ault owners.

She really enjoyed living in Ault. She had acquired a large clientele of customers and didn't want to abandon them and the owners who treated her with great respect. So decisions, decisions, she felt that she had quite a dilemma to overcome. Well history tells us that it was only fate that she would accept the job in Fort Lupton at the Half Moon Café.

Fort Lupton was quite a bit closer to Denver where others cousins had migrated from New Mexico. Her closest cousin happened to live in Brighton who happened to be Conrado Gonzales, who happened to be married to Mom's Sister Rosie Chacon.

One day Eddie Chacon had been visiting his sister Rose in Brighton. Eddie was in search of a Mrs. Eddie Chacon. Rose and Conrado thought that Eddie and Erminda would be a great couple. Conrado invited Eddie to go visit Erminda had the Half Moon café to have lunch. Eddie was somewhat reluctant at first, but finally went to visit Erminda at the Half Moon.

"Hey Lalo, I want to introduce you to my cousin from New Mexico, her name is Erminda Quintana, pleaded Conrado, I think you'll be pleased to meet her."

Eddie's nickname was Lalo and thus the story tells us that they made their way to Fort Lupton to meet this Miss Quintana.

"Now look Lalo, don't worry about a thing I'll do all of the talking," assured Conrado.

"Okay Conrado I have all the faith in the world that this Miss Quintana will be the one in my future," said Eddie.

When they arrived at the Half moon café, Eddie and Conrado were directed to their table. Eddie seemed somewhat apprehensive, but was overcome by her presence when he first set his eyes on her.

"Hi Erminda, I wanted to introduce you to my *cunado* (brother-in-law) Eddie Chacon from Denver. His sister Mary so happens to be married to your cousin Jose Elijio Quintana from Variadero, New Mexico," said Conrado. His half sister is your Aunt Josefita.

"I've heard of Elijio but don't really know him that much. I heard he got married to a Chacon, but I didn't realize that she had a brother," said Erminda. "Well Eddie, it's a pleasure to meet you."

Then Erminda walked away quickly to attend to her other customers. As the two young men ate their food, she occasionally would take a glimpse at this young caballero who wanted to meet her.

As they left the premises Conrado walked up to Erminda and said that Eddie wanted to go on a date with her. She told Conrado that she'd think about it and it would be nice if Eddie could come back and visit her at the café next week.

So history tells us that Eddie made his way back to the Half moon on several more occasions. They dated for 4 months. On December 10th 1952 they became Mr. and Mrs. Eddie Chacon and were married in Villanueva, New Mexico.

Chapter 30

My Parents Names are Mary and Joseph

I am the son of a rancher and the son of a migrant farm worker...

How coincidental, my parent's names are Mary and Joseph. I never really thought of it, but wella! This can only be the beginning of something good a precedent to life. What if, at the time of naming me? Oh that would have never happened... Well let's continue the story.

The year was 1952 and Joe had been working for about a year at United Fryars and Stillmans. Back in New Mexico opportunity arose and Joe and Mary found themselves moving back Las Vegas, New Mexico, running a little dry goods store. Joe took a year leave of absence from the packing house and wanted to give the market business a shot.

I was born about 11 months earlier, Albert Cruz Quintana on January 16th 1953. I guess you can say that I was lucky to be born from such fine parents. I was born the son of a rancher and a migrant farm worker, what a great combination. Both come from very hard working philosophies of life.

Dad loved New Mexico, especially the ranch. From Denver he made frequent visits to his Mom's every 3 months. Grandpa Quintana had passed away in 1948. So Dad made it a routine to visit the ranch once every 3 months. Grandma loved Mom and was so happy that her son married such a good lady. Mom would help Grandma with all of the chores. Living on the ranch was always a lot of hard work. When Mom would visit, she helped Grandma quite a bit.

History tells us that Joe wasn't a very good entrepreneur. The people who traded there at the dry goods, all wanted credit and wouldn't pay off their bills. So the idea of taking a year off from the packing house was a very good idea. Therefore, as the migrant farm worker knows so well, pick up pack and move.

Months later in search of their dream home, Mom and Dad fell in love with a little suburb town outside of Denver to live. It was in proximity of Dad's work, about 4 miles north of Denver. Derby was its name; it was the ideal place to raise a family. During those first years in Derby, Bernadine and Michael were born.

Mom was a great house wife, fulfilling all that was expected of her. She was the prototype of all moms. Not only did she keep a very clean house, she made sure that Dad always had a hot breakfast in the morning before work and always made sure that her children were clean and fed. She was a volunteer room mother for all of her three kids and also volunteered as a den mother for cub scouts. Yes life was sure good in Derby. We sure loved it. Could it get any better?

Chapter 31

Super Mom

After six years of living in Derby, Dad got a wild hair up his derrière and wanted to span his horizons and bought an old abandoned creamery off of 60th and Washington in the Globeville section of Denver. Dad's dream was to convert this creamery into a Mexican American restaurant. It just seemed as if Dad was never satisfied with what good he had going. Mom was always there to support and never really questioned Dad's motives, but there she was sweeping, scrubbing and working off her tail to help start this restaurant.

"Mary, it's time to leave Derby, we'll rent out the house and we can move into the living quarters of the creamery while we do all of the renovation of the restaurant," said Joe as he pulled out the blue prints to show Mary. "I'll continue to work at the packing house while the construction is in process. This will give us a consistent cash flow so we won't go under."

"Okay honey whatever you want done, I support you 100%," responded Mary as she looked at the detail of the prints.

Sure enough Dad and Mom moved the entire family into the living quarters of the creamery, located in the back rooms of the building. While all of the construction was taking place in the front of the new restaurant it made for a very dangerous environment for kids to be in and around. The front of the building was off limits to the children.

One day Mom took the children to the front room of the building to see how much construction had taken place. Then the phone rang so

Mom ran to answer the phone in the back. There we were, left by ourselves to play in a danger zone. I was 6, Bernadine was 5 and Michael was 2. Bernadine and I were very curious, looking around. Michael sat on the floor playing with the saw dust and wooden two by four blocks. When Mom went to the back to answer the phone Bernadine was very curious when she saw a conduit pole coming upwards from the floor. Her curiosity got the better of her and finally she grabbed the pole and then a volt of electricity bolted through her body. Bernadine's feet left the ground while her hands clinched the pole and then her little body was swiveling around the pole in robotic fashion. I saw her with her feet mid air and ran to grab her. Then, I too was part of this circling motion. All I can remember was screaming for Mom's help. Every time I said help, my voice came out stuttering as if I was being punched in the mouth every second over and over again. It seemed as if we were going to die when Mom finally heard the plea and came into the room running as fast as an Olympic sprinter. When she saw us spinning around the pole amid the electrical current she had no time to think, but act. She threw her whole body horizontally at the pole and broke the current. She looked like a middle line backer with her total body extended, tackling the exposed electric pole. After Mom broke the current both Bernadine and I flew in two different directions of the room. The hair on our heads was on end and Bernadine's lips were purple. When I spoke, smoke came from my mouth.

I'll always remember that day when my Mom saved our lives. Yes, she's a super mom alright, she's the greatest. When Dad got home from work he found out that the wires were live and should have been taped or maybe the electricity should have been shut off. That evening Dad fired the electrician and hired a new one to finish the job.

Finally, the day came, the grand opening of our restaurant, Quintana Roo. What a proud day it was for Dad. It was his dream to live the dream and to get rich. Again, Mom was there to support him. But still Dad was working at the packing house just in case.

Then Dad was dealt some bad cards when his mom, Grandma Delfinia passed away. It seemed as if this really changed Dad. He wasn't the same. He became very bitter and his abuse of alcohol started. Dad was so different. He was not the same man. He wasn't the kind of guy that would open up to Mom, for he saw that as a sign of weakness. He had many episodes where he would come home drunk and Mom was left to run the restaurant. He was a mess. They hired help that couldn't be trusted and were being robbed, when Mom wasn't looking.

I hated the new school in Denver and cried daily not wanting to go. Mom was pivotal in having us move down the street to a duplex in a real neighborhood. From here we changed schools. This is where I had great experience in a parochial school. This is where I learned to be a student.

But as history tells us that Dad wasn't the great entrepreneur that he hoped to be. Dad lost the restaurant and we now were on our way back to our old home in Derby.

The day that we went back to our home in Derby, had to be one of the happiest days of my life. I missed the school I originally went to and all the neighbors and friends. Derby was an awesome community to grow up in and Mom was in her element the, as a house wife.

Mom was always so giving and gracious. I can remember one time in high school; the Spanish club was promoting a field trip to Mexico City. Mom was just laid off her job and was only getting unemployment. Her unemployment wasn't much, but she gave me the money from the check which allowed me to go. The rest of the month we suffered and just ate beans and potatoes the whole month. But Mom always made the beans and potatoes so delicious. It always seemed as if we were very poor. Dad was making lots of money, but the priority was his drink. Mom knew that this trip to Mexico City was important to me. It's easy to tell your kids we have no money for certain things. But Mom knew that this trip could mean a life changing experience for my success. She always was so sensitive to our needs. I guess it's called motherly instinct.

As the years passed we all were fortunate to have graduated from Adams City High School. I continued through to college and received my Bachelor's degree from the University of Northern Colorado. This is where I met my wife Louise. We both became teachers and later received our Masters at the University of Colorado at Boulder. My sister Bernadine got married and was a house wife raising her 3 children, while her husband worked at the City of Boulder. Michael, our younger brother became a welder and married a Commerce City girl who was a worker at a local cookie and pastry factory and had 3 children.

During the time I was in college Dad's abuse of alcohol worsen. He was very abusive and Mom was a nervous wreck. He became very physically abusive and at times we had to put him in rehab. We too the children, lived an at-risk life. Sometimes our friends weren't the best people to hang out with. So when I was off to college the dysfunction of our home was at its peak. They were all drinking and smoking and partying like it was the end of the world. Mom was at home and had to go through all of this

42

turmoil. I tried to lecture my brother and sister but it went in one ear and out the other. Experience had to teach them the lesson of life.

I don't know how Mom survived all the abuse and unruly children. All I know is that she always put her whole faith in God. She was always upbeat and always gave people a sense of hope. She loved to laugh and have a lot of fun.

I'll always remember one Fourth of July when we were very young. As children we were all excited about the fireworks and the celebration. The Fourth of July picnic in Greeley was where we wanted to spend our 4th. On the 3rd of July, Dad was arrested and thrown in jail for driving under the influence of alcohol and our celebration was ruined. But Mom always had a way to cheer us up. We had our own picnic in the front yard with the best food Mom could prepare. That Fourth, she made the best green chili Mexican hamburgers I'd ever eaten. Yes, Mom is truly a "Super Mom."

Chapter 32

Chile Verde, Mom's Gift to Us

In all of this depression came something very positive from Mom and Quintana Roo, green chili, yes green chili, chile' verde. Quintana Roo had the best green chili south of Aztlan. This is where Mom learned how to cook this family heirloom. She learned to make this sacred dish from a little lady from Guanajuato, Mexico, who was hired as a cook at Quintana Roo. From 1960 to the present Mom has made this dish with the correct amount of ingredients. A little bit of this and a touch of that. But the greatest ingredient is a big pinch of love.

This cuisine was magical and could work great wonders for all. Along with this magical dish was served a fresh warm tortilla and a big bowl of frijoles. This magical cuisine has been eaten throughout the generations, from Moctezuma to César Chavez. Now that's eating with great company, do you agree?

Where we lived on 77th place in Derby, which later became Commerce City, Mom's green chili burritos were a hit. Everyone would want some of Mom's green chili. The neighborhood kids would come by and hang around and wait for the invite for a burrito or two. If the neighbor kids were lucky Mom would tell stories about growing up as a migrant farm worker in Weld and Larimer Counties.

When their parents heard about Mom's green chili they wanted her recipe, for all their children had a craving for. She tried to teach them, but she never gave them that one secret ingredient. Many learned to roll the tortilla and boil the bean and refry, but the chile verde could not be duplicated.

Occasions were always the best time to prepare this magical food. For Thanksgiving and Christmas you'd hear about someone's cranberry sauce or turkey stuffing but on our holidays it was turkey or ham with, you guessed it, green chili.

Mom is a very gifted chef, she is so good that she didn't know that her chile' was even therapeutic. In times of trouble it seemed as if a nice bowl of chile' verde and bowl of frijoles with a freshly made tortilla could chase the blues away.

In terms of a legacy this magical food was also made by Mom's children. It will be passed on to the upcoming generations. Have you guessed yet that I'm loco over Mom's cooking, especially her green chili... I'm craving it right now... I'm salivating... I'm sure getting hungry... Vamos a la cena... Come to the supper table...

Chapter 33

Mom,
A True Prayer Warrior

Intercessory prayer has been a tradition in our family for generations as you've read. Whenever anyone was facing some any sort of ordeal or tragedy or maybe just giving thanks to God, Mom would be catalyst and asked by the parties to pray for them. Her love for Jesus came through the recitation and meditation of the Rosary. Religiously speaking she would say her prayers daily for the intentions of those who needed prayer.

Growing up Mom made it a tradition to pray the Rosary before we went to bed. Our prayers were very strong during the time of the Cold war. The Cuban Missile Crises was the time we prayed the most. During the time that John F. Kennedy was able to dismantle diplomatically the threat of nuclear war in the western hemisphere. I truly believe it was all the prayers that helped the President do so.

Grandpa Henry was a long time democrat and true follower of J.F.K and wrote a story about his tragic assassination. There was such a love by our people for the only Roman Catholic President in our history. I remember that it sure was a sad day for our family. Even at an old age Grandpa Henry was writing poetry and worship praises (alabados). I truly believe that it was his example that was passed on to love the Lord and of course the example of Manuelita as she pulled out her Rosary on many occasions. Who can forget about the silver Rosary that tied their marriage together?

I still remember friends wanting to stay overnight. But before they would come over they'd ask if we were praying a Rosary. If we were, then they'd make an excuse and say that they forgot that they had something to do. You see when you pray the Rosary it is a very patient prayer but physically demanding, because you had to pray it on your knees. To ask a young child to pray for 20 minutes on their knees was asking a lot. But in any tragedy or turmoil pull out your beads and pray with your whole heart and the pain of kneeling will leave your body. Mom always felt that a little sacrifice would be the key to a miracle. This was her faith in God working.

During the Vietnam War, Aunt Rosie had three sons who protected our freedoms; Felix, Leroy and Raymond. Mom had us pray every night for their safety and well being. Mom had a big heart and really was empathetic to her sister who feared for her sons' lives. God was great because all three sons were able to come back with honors. Felix accomplished two tours in Nam and served as a Staff Sergeant. Everyone was so proud of them. Aunt Rosie was so happy and thanked Mom for all the prayers.

You see Mom's love for the Rosary came at a very early age. So early, that Mom was still in the womb of her mother. Grandma Manuelita had been carrying Mom very low throughout the pregnancy. Manuelita had been feeling ill and prayed constantly that someone would heal her. Of course her method of prayer was the Holy Rosary. About in the second trimester of the pregnancy she could not stand the pain anymore so she went to the doctor and he too, had given up hope. They all felt that there would be a miscarriage. But miraculously speaking, a medicine man who happened to be a Ute Indian and his wife showed up at Manuelita's front door selling of all sorts of herbs. She had shared with them that she'd been ill and was ready to deliver in 3 months and she was afraid to lose the baby. They prescribed a special herb so she would feel better. After ingesting the herb, instantaneously, Manuelita was feeling great and delivered Mom 3 months later with no complications on March 26th 1927. Manuelita and Henry were so happy and thankful that God had sent a messenger to heal her. Several days later another girl from Eaton was experiencing a problem similar to Manuelita's. The Indian couple was nowhere to be found in the north. Many people in the community felt that the two Indians were angels sent to save Manuelita and my Mom.

Another example of her love for our Lord and La Virgen came when she gave birth to my younger sister Bernadine. Mom had had a bad fall when she was pregnant. One day she was washing clothes and slipped on a wet spot on the floor. Repercussions occurred and Mom was rushed to the hospital. Instantly, she went into labor. Her pain was so severe that they had to give her ether gas to deal with the pain. The doctor felt the baby turn and Mom let out a scream, then the doctor said, "The baby's breeched." Then Mom cried out so that God would heal her pain.

As she screamed out she looked above the light on the ceiling of the delivery room, El Santo Niño de Atocha appeared. Mom said that after she saw the baby Jesus, she was assured that it was a sign that all was going to be fine. Now if you study any religious history you'd know that in Spain in the 1500's when a woman was ready to give birth, a statue of Santo Nino de Atocha was borrowed from the Church and taken to the home of the pregnant girl. This would help assist with the birth of the baby. In Spain at Atocha, the baby statue was detachable from the statue of the Blessed Virgen. This allowed for the devout Christians to borrow the statue of the baby Jesus during the time of births as needed. Now I know that Mom never studied the religious significance of the baby Jesus, but her vision was the reality at the birth of Bernadine. You be the judge.

Now Mom is a prayer warrior on many prayer chains in the church. I believe that she has a special gift given to her by God. Most people in time of need call Mom for intercessory prayer. Believe me Mom's prayers are powerful.

But the most memorable time Mom's prayers came through is when her grandson Javier my son got hurt in a football accident. This is where we waited for a miracle.

It was probably one of the worst days in our lives. With six minutes left in the football game, number 24 laid face down on the ground. In a matter of minutes we were on an ambulance on our way to University Hospital. Javier was laying in the emergency room waiting for a prognosis.

Up to this game Javier was one of the best high school football players in the state. After the first three games of the season he had over 50 tackles. His main goal after graduation was wrestle and play football in college. He'd been wrestling since he was five and playing football since he was eight.

The next day we waited for the diagnosis. There was set of doctors who came in to evaluate him. The main doctor of the group said he would never be able to play football again, but there would be a chance that he could wrestle. Javier was totally devastated; his dreams were dying before him. On the third day Louise and I were not able to get to the hospital early. When we arrived that morning, my sister Bernadine was waiting there with Javy. The main neurosurgeon had told him that morning that he would never wrestle again. When we got the news Louise and I broke down. The doctor didn't seem very sympathetic, so I argued that one of the other doctors said he could wrestle while you said he couldn't. There had to be some mix-up. In addition, the doctor said he had Congenitive Stenosis (born with a narrow spinal column), and if he'd get another severe blow to the head he would be paralyzed for life. The doctor left the room and then my next move was to call Mom, the prayer warrior. Mom immediately went to work and pulled out her Rosary. We too dropped to our knees and prayed for a healing.

The next news from the doctor was that Javier would need surgery to widen the spinal column around the neck area. In our estimation this didn't make sense. He'd been playing football and wrestled for years and never complained about his neck. So as a cautious father I told the doctor that no one is cutting into my son's neck! "I want a second opinion!"

Well, the news got worse; our insurance wouldn't cover the surgery in that hospital, so we had to switch to our insurance surgeons. The next surgeon also wanted to dig into his neck. I completely lost my composure and told the surgeon he was nuts. This wasn't a pleasant time in the Quintana family. Louise and I were at odds and our discussions were not too pleasant to hear.

So my next move was to get another opinion, so I took him to a spinal doctor. I showed him the x-rays and the MRI films. He examined the films and said, "Yes there was some stenosis but the body has a way to heal itself. You have to let the Lord do His job." This special doctor reminded me of the days when all the doctors of the north diagnosed Uncle Johnny with Tuberculosis and in reality he had an old injury that had to be cleaned internally. Could history be repeating itself?

This special doctor, referred us to other doctors, but they wouldn't take second opinion cases, for fear of lawsuits. What happened to the Hippocratic Oath? What I liked most about our special doctor is that he went over the films with us point by point and that he too had a special faith in God's healing power.

All during this time Mom continued to pray relentlessly. She would call us periodically and check on her grandson's health. She also asked other's to pray at the Ultreyas and prayer meetings at church. She prayed unceasingly.

Spiritually speaking, I was getting a message, to believe and have faith in Him before having faith in man. Wow how profound! This was something Mom always taught us children, to have faith...

Well, to make a long story short, Javier's personal doctor decision left the final decision to us. By the Grace of God and all of the prayers through the community and Mom, Javier completed the wrestling season with no neck pain. In fact he had an exemplary season. He was the Grand Champion at the Adams County Tourney, runner up at the Weld County Tourney, champion at the Moffat County Dog Fight Tourney, 5th place finisher at the University of Northern Colorado Tourney (48 teams participated), Champion at the Sterling Tourney, Region I Champion at Greeley where he defeated the #1 ranked 215 lb'r in State and finally finished 4th in State against the best in Colorado. He finished the year by making the All Colorado freestyle team that competed in Oklahoma.

Yes Mom's prayer was very instrumental in Javier's healing and all I can do is thank her for the healing and hats off to the special spine doctor who had great faith in the Lord. These are only a few examples of what Mom has done for her friends and family.

Chapter 34

A Renaissance Period

A week after Dad's funeral his older brother Augustine and his wife came to Mom's home give their condolences. Remember he never attended his own brother's funeral services. I was very sad and hurt with my oldest uncle. I hardly had anything to say to the man. Business before family is always a bad policy. All I know is that I was now the leader of our family and was going to try my best to make the best home for my family and Mom.

Times were very hard during the grieving process. Mom was always strong and really never showed too much emotion. For the upcoming months she kept herself busy with the Charismatic Prayer Group at the Church and also participated in the Cursillo Movement. Both Movements of the Church were very supportive in helping us heal our loss.

Then the willingness to succeed and be proficient were her goals, she was motivated. Bernadine and I worked on building Mom's self esteem and confidence. It all started with something as simple as learning to keep a check book balanced. That sounds fundamental, but Dad handled all of the finances. All Mom had to worry about was the house keeping and the children. But after Dad passed, she had to be responsible for everything. It seemed that in the old days fathers expected their daughters to marry good men who were great providers. But in the 20th and 21st centuries women are expected to have careers.

So therefore Mom went through a renaissance period, a rebirth, resurgence in life. She learned quickly with very little coaching. She was driving her own vehicle all over the metro area. She was giving testimonials at the prayer meetings and Cursillo Ultreyas. On Sundays she was singing in the church choir. You could see a spark of confidence. Everyone complimented her on her singing. Now she had a skip in her walk. Before she was ridiculed for anything she did by her husband who never encouraged her to prosper. Well today we all know that it was the booze talking. Addiction affects everyone that's within its circle. But after years of abuse, Mom would have to dig deep to overcome the disease of being the wife of an alcoholic.

Mom has to acknowledge the legacy set forth by her rich culture, what it meant to be a Chacon, Duran and eventually a Quintana. Chili loses it essence when it has no spice to it. This time of renaissance was when Mom reached her potential. It's like when she was a little girl singing on the radio station in front an audience of thousands and bringing home the blue ribbon. This is when she was like gold, singing with so much *orgullo*, (pride) confidence and joy.

Chapter 35

Mom in the Future, the Ideal Man

Now that Mom has all of this confidence what will the future bring? Well, at age 60 she's still young enough to get remarried and have a very happy life. Who will the lucky guy be? I want to mold the perfect man for my Mother. Here is that prototype.

He must be a man of God, who follows the doctrine of the Holy Roman Catholic Church. This means that he must be well versed in the Holy Scriptures of the Bible. His example must be exemplary as a very positive role model in the Church and Community. He must be a member of the Cursillo Movement evangelizing the world for Jesus.

Above all, he must be honest and trustworthy. Dad used to just take off and never would tell Mom where he was going. This is a big "NO NO" and should not be tolerated by anyone. No single vacations! They should always be together on vacations.

Mary's family must be a big part of his life as his children are a part of her life. When functions are in the interest of each party they too must show respect and attend. In other words you marry the entire family. In times of trouble this man must be empathetic to her needs. He must help her cook and clean as necessary. Complimenting her cooking would be a smart idea, especially her green chili. When a family member is in need of trouble the help will come with total humility and generosity.

He must compliment her on her cooking and singing and too must be musically inclined. Music is such a big part of mom's life. This ideal man must play the guitar and sing duets with her. His demeanor is one of honesty and supports mom in all musical endeavors.

When promises are made they must be followed through. Empty promises are killers to relationships. I would expect this prototype to take mom on Mediterranean cruises, trips to the orient, the Holy Land and of course the Vatican. Trips to neighboring states just don't cut it for they are only trips that are expected to take in respect to familial functions.

This person must have sense of tolerance, the ability to respect people's views even if they are different. Regardless of ethnicity this person should not judge people by the color of their skin. When addressing people they must address them by who they are and not, the Italiano, Mexican, Pole or Colored. This indirectness is a sign of disrespect and cannot be tolerated and shows ignorance.

The use and abuse of alcohol cannot be a part of the ideal prototype of the perfect husband. Alcohol is a dangerous agent that cripples families and lives. Not even one is a good policy, for its example is poor at best.

First and foremost this prototype of a perfect husband must love my Mother with a love that puts her first above everything else because this is what she deserves, only the best. Now is this asking too much for such a great Lady.

I don't know how true it is but what I heard through the grapevine is that she met this certain guy through a singles' group. I sure hope that he meets my criteria of the most perfect husband for my dearest Mother. She is the center of her family's life. I sure hope that she does not forget that she is our heart. Without our Mother, there is no more, green chili. *No hay chile verde.*

Mom, this is your legacy, it is filled with so much to be proud of. Your history is so valuable. The people of your lineage have created Colorado history at its finest. This alone is enough to tell the world that you are of nobility. That same nobility runs through the veins of all your children and grandchildren. We too can now see our heritage through the stories of our ancestors.

Now the days of Fernando Duran, Félix Duran, Juan Chacón, Gracia Duran, Eloísa Chacón, Eduardo Chacón, Eduardo Duran, Chencho Duran, Aurora Duran, Genoeva Duran, Ramón Duran, Jesucita Duran, Enrique Chacón, Manuelita Duran, Rosie Chacón, Eddie Chacón are no longer with us, but their legacy will live on.

The end…

Alabados and Poetry

By Enrique Henry Chacon
Translations and edit set up by Bea Montoya, Linda Dale Jennings and Albert Quintana. Alabado retrieval by Anna Alires Gonzales Chacon daughter of Rose Chacon

As read previously, we learned about Henry Chacon's poetic and storytelling talent. He'd only attended public schools to the first grade. With such a minute education he was able to conjure up some pretty eloquent poetry. Henry's involvement in the Penitente Movement, the Brotherhood was what taught him to love and praise God though the Alabados, hymnal praises, a style indicative of the Penitentes of Northern New Mexico and Southern Colorado.

His character can also attribute to his prowess. He was able to converse with anyone. In the time he lived in Fountain, Colorado he befriended Antonio Villani. Henry was able to converse with him in Italian and when he worked with the Germans in northern Colorado he was also able to speak in German let alone English and his first language Spanish.

Henry was famous for his despedimientos or alabados known as farewell songs chanted in unison at wakes and funerals. He was also able to present entrega or rite of passage at weddings where the father of a bride gives the daughter away with a blessing. He sung and or chanted the alabados a capella. Sometimes he'd use a pito, a flute-like instrument which evoked sounds that were very eerie. His explanation was that it was the poor souls in Purgatory crying out for forgiveness. He also said that it was the cry of the Blessed Virgin for Jesus at the Via de La Rosa during the crucifixion.

During Lent and on special occasions the Penitentes would sing in unison to symbolize the unity of the Brotherhood. The sound of an alabado ceremony at a wake and funeral was very distinct. The sound

185

was comparable to the lower tones of a bag pipe. The men evoked the sound which would blow through the Morada. It also sounded similar to a Powwow, where the braves would repeat the sounds in a very low tone. The word to describe this was melismatic, making the voice quaver like that of Arabic and Jewish music, but with a booming resonance.

As a young boy staying over Grandpa and Grandma Chacons, I would peruse through the multitude of notebooks of Grandpa's poetry and literature. It never really mattered what color of pen he used. What pen he found would do the trick. If he had a thought he'd write it down in red, pink, yellow, purple whatever color of pen was in his reach. I couldn't read it because I didn't have the skill in interpreting his Spanish poetry.

I can vaguely recall him, once at a wedding, singing an entrega, where he would recite poetry that was dedicated to the two who were just married. The parents of the bride and groom would both kneel down in front of their parents. The words of the entrega would touch the people so deeply that there was not a dry eye at the reception. This entrega was a formal blessing, a rite of passage to adulthood that would send the new couple into their future.

In the following pages you'll see Henry's alabados written at their finest. They will illustrate Henry Chacon's art at their best. The first alabado is entitled Alabado I, it is a general prayer of thanksgiving. This type of prayer was traditional prayer prayed at the Morada or chapel where the Penitentes would recite their prayers during the Lenten season of the Catholic Church. It is written in its original Spanish text and then translated in English.

Alabado II is about getting through the gates of heaven by means of St. Peter. This alabado focuses on God's trust in St. Peter. It is an example of a despedimiento recited at wakes.

Alabado III is a tribute to St. Francis of Assisi, the patron saint of the Penitente Movement. It also points out the tragedy of death and how it can be overcome by the belief in Jesus Christ.

The last piece is not an alabado but a poem. This poem is entitled, The Assassination of John F. Kennedy. Henry had a great love for JFK. When Kennedy was killed it was a very traumatic time for him. Henry always talked about how JFK was able to dismantle the missiles in Cuba. Many Rosaries were prayed at this time and the results were evident when Fidel Castro ceased fire as a consequence of the diplomacy of such a great president.

Enjoy these alabados and poetry they are truly a treasure and represent the best to come out of Colorado and the Southwest. It's just a little bit of history that never gets told.

Albert Quintana a native Coloradoan comes to the media scene with over 30 years' experience as a social studies teacher in the public school system. His forte' is historical narration. In short he is a great story teller. This is attributed to his years of experience working with inner city youth, where he made history come alive.

His role model was his mother where she told him the interesting stories about being a migrant farm worker in Larimer and Weld Counties in Northern Colorado, as depicted in, No More Green Chili.

His first book was, A Teacher Grows up in Commerce City, published in 2003. This book is his autobiography about growing up in a town in northern Denver Metro area the 1960's. Assimilation, acculturation and the struggle for cultural identity are the themes of this book.

Alabados #1
By Enrique Chacón

1.
Bendice Señor la cena
en la mesa del altar
y echemos su bendición
Como Padre celestial…

2.
Este sagrado convite
en la mesa del altar
es la cena del Señor
En la corte celestial…

3.
La bendición de Dios padre
hecho omnipotente
en esta Santa Morada
Desde cuerpo de tu gente…

4.
Padre bendice a su pueblo
que te pide contrición
en esta Santa Morada
Echemos su bendición…

5.
El jueves Santo en la noche a
todos los comulgó entre dientes
de pan su cuerpo nos dio…

6.
Y al mismo tiempo les dijo
que había de experimentar
que en aquella misma noche
todos lo habían de dejar…

1.
Lord, bless this supper placed
on the table of your altar.
We ask for your blessings,
celestial Father that you are.

2.
This blessed banquet on the table
of your alter is the supper of the
Lord from they celestial harvest.

3.
The blessings of our father create
omnipotence in this Holy Morada
from the body of His people.

4.
Father, Bless this community
who begs for forgiveness. In
your Holy name we give this
Holy Morada Blessing.

5.
On Holy Thursday in the
evening He gave communion
to all of us, through bits of
bread He gave us His body.

6.
At the same time, He told them
that same night they would all
abandon Him. (He's talking
about Holy Thursday when
they met for the Last supper.)

7.

San Pedro que aquí está
ya le cupo un gran pesar
Señor bendice la cena
En la mesa del altar…

8.

Con el bello de Jesús
le vamos a acompañar
en la Santa Morada
Y en la mesa del altar…

9.

Por las ánimas benditas
Debemos todos rogar
En esta Santa Morada
En la mesa del altar…

10.

Señor en esta Santa Morada
Nos diste el alimento
sin merecerlo
Echemos tu bendición…
Amen
Gracias te damos Señor…

7.

St. Peter who was there felt a
great weight. Lord, Bless this
supper on the table of your altar.

8.

With the beauty of Jesus we will
accompany Him on the Holy
Morada and the table of the altar.

8.

With Jesus' beauty we accompany
him to the His Holy Chapel
and to His Holy altar

9.

For the blessed souls of purgatory,
we should pray in this Holy
Morada and the table of the altar.

10.

Lord, in this Holy Morada
you've given us the strength even
though we are not worthy of
it. Lord, gives your blessing.
Amen we give thanks to the Lord!

Alabados #2
By Enrique Chacón

1.
Las llaves del cielo son
a San Pedro encomendadas
para toditas las almas que valen
De Dios selladas…

2.
Por un Dios verdadero
que así lo determinó
a San Pedro escogió
Para portero del cielo…

3.
En vida puedan buscar
las almas este remedio
a San Pedro lo han de aclamar
Como puertero del cielo…

4.
Las almas que van ayudadas
por un Dios muy verdadero
y a San Pedro presentado
Porque es portero del cielo…

5.
A las almas más confiadas
a un sólo Dios verdadero
y a San Pedro presentadas
Como portero del cielo…

6.
Las almas que van confiadas
A un sólo Dios verdadero
y San Pedro las recibe
Para lo eterno del cielo…

1.
The keys to heaven are entrusted
to St. Peter for all souls who
value God's Holy seal

2.
Our true God determined that
St. Peter should be the gatekeeper
of heaven, so He chose him.

3.
In life, souls might look for this
remedy and acclaim and pray to St.
Peter, since he is the gatekeeper.

4.
The souls most helped by our
own true God are the ones
that acclaim St. Peter as the
gatekeeper of heaven.

5.
The most trusting souls in our
one true God believe that St.
Peter is the gatekeeper of heaven.

6.
The souls who believe in one
true God, St. Peter will Receive
them to the eternity of heaven.

7.

Ay, Dios está mirando
de las almas su vivir
y San Pedro está esperando
a las que ha de recibir...

8.

Que gran favor mereció
San Pedro, Dios verdadero
por el Señor lo nombró
Como portero del cielo...

9.

En fin, no santo agraciado
te pidamos con gran celo
de corazón abrazado,
Abras las puertas del cielo...

7.

Aye, God is watching souls of
Lives and St. Peter is waiting
for those he will receive.

8.

What great favor he deserved,
our true God name St. Peter
as the gatekeeper of heaven.

9.

In the end, the Lord graced him
with the coveted role. We pray with
great ardor, our hearts embraced,
open the gates to heaven.

Alabados #3

By Enrique Chacón

1.

Ayudar almas queridas
a sentir a vuestro Padre
que es mi Jesús Nazareno
De la Virgen Madre…

2.

Allí lo ven en altar
come piadoso y bendito
pidiendo misericordia
El gloriosa San Francisco…

3.

Ya lo ven con su mar taza
Y con su cuerda.
Lo han visto echando
sus bendiciones
El glorioso, San Francisco…

4.

Y a San Antonio lo guía
con su sagrado niñito
a que conceda el milagro,
El glorioso San Francisco…

5.

Allí lo ven en la gloria
limpiándole el rostro a Cristo
con la túnica sagrada
El glorioso San Francisco…

6.

San José en sus días y noches
con sus milagros benditos
le pide aquellos rosarios
Al glorioso San Francisco…

1.

Helping dear souls to feel our
father who is my Jesus of Nazareth,
son of the Virgin Mother!

2.

There you see him at the altar,
pious and holy, asking for mercy,
the glorious San Francisco.

3.

There you see him with his (mar
taza!) and with his rope. They
have seen him giving his blessings,
the glorious, San Francisco.

4.

And San Antonio guides
with his sacred baby Jesus,
He grants us miracles, The
glorious San Francisco.

5.

There you see him in the
glory, cleaning the face of
Christ with his sacred tunic,
the glorious San Francisco

6.

Saint Joseph with his blessed
miracles asks for rosaries day and
night, the glorious San Francisco.

7.

Ya llega la Santa Muerte
en figura de abnegada
a defender esta causa
Del Señor sacramentado…

8.

Ese camino de Dios
lo ponen crucificado
ahí lo anduvo de rodillas
mi comadre Celestina… con
niña hachita en las manos
A llevarse a los mortales…

9.

La Santa Muerte salió
paseándose en su carreta
con las órdenes de Dios
a las almas representa…

10.

Ya salió la Santa Muerte
a recitar al enfermo
a encomardale a Dios
y líbralo del infierno…

11.

Ya salió la Santa Muerte
con sus órdenes legales
con su flechita en la mano
a llevarse a los mortales…

12.

La Santa Muerte
salía por el mundo y por los mares
con su cuerdita en las manos
a llevarse a los mortales…

7.

Then came His Death, in the form
of a martyr to defend the Lord's
sacred cause. Our Sacred Lord.

8.

God's path drove Him to the
crucifixion, the path he crawled
on His knees, my celestial friend.

9.

Then Holy Death went out,
riding in her cart with orders
from God to represent all souls.

10.

Holy Death goes out to recite
to the sick, to pray for them to
God and free them from hell.

11.

Holy Death goes out with
her legal order, with bow
and arrow in hand, to take
Hawaii those mortals.

12.

Holy Death traveled the
World and through the oceans
with her hope in her hands
to take away the mortals.

13.

La Santa Muerte salía
con la cruz y sus orales
con niña hachita en las manos
A llevarse a los mortales…

14.

Ya lo ponen en la cruz
ya da sus cuentos cabales
cumpliendo sus testamentos
Y llevándose a los mortales…

15.

En el Calvario
la ven en su carreta
sentada pidiendo su limosnita
mi comadre Sebestiana…

16.

Y a le rezan su sudario en
el calvario postrada y le
echan mi bendicion mi
comadre Sebestiana…

17.

Los esclavos de Jesús son
los que la acompañaban
En su sagrada pasión mi
compadre Sebestiana…

18.

Cuarenta dias anduvo en
su carreta postrada
Acompañando a Jesús
mi comadre S
Sebestiana…

19.

Y a lo suben con cadenas con
mi marrada a que los bendiga
Dios mi comadre Sebestiana…

13.

Holy Death traveled with her cross
and prayers, with a small ax in
hand to take away the mortals.

14.

They put him on the cross;
He tells her horrific story,
completing his testament and
taking the mortals with him.

15.

At Calvary you see her sitting
in her cart, begging for alms,
my comadre Sebestiana.

16.

In Calgary, prostrated with
exhortation, they pray that she rest
in peace and they give her their
blessings, comadre Sebestiana.

17.

Jesus' servants are the ones that
accompanied her in her sacred
passion, comadre Sebestiana.

18.

Forty days she traveled prostrated
on her cart, accompanying
Jesus comadre Sebestiana.

19.

They raised Him up with
chains may God bless them,
comadre Sebestiana.

20.

Jesús, Jesús de mi vida
Ándale las tres vaqueados
con una vela en la mano
Mi comadre Sebestiana…

21.

Jesús, Jesús de mi vida
Ándale las tres vaqueados
con una vela en la mano
Mi comadre Sebestiana…

22.

Y a la ven martajas el
paciente te reclama
Para clavar su cajón
Mi comadre Sebestiana…

23.

El Señor la llama para que
lleve aquella alma,
Con su espadita en la mano
Mi comadre Sebestiana…

24.

¿Dónde va San Juan Bautista
Con el Señor caminando.
esperando a sus pacientes
Que para el cielo va guiando…

25.

¿Dónde va el Niño perdido
con su túnica morada
y su corona de espinas
y la sangre en sus espaldas…

26.

Ya lo llevan
Por la calle de amargura.
atado de pies y manos
Amando a la colonia

20.

Jesus, The Jesus of my life
with candles in hand, follow
my comadre Sebestiana.

21.

Jesus, The Jesus of my life,
with candles in hand, follow
comadre Sebestiana.

22.

The patient chains that he has
seen nailing down their coffin
my comadre Sebestiana…

23.

The Lord calls her so she can take
that soul with her and her bow and
arrow in hand comadre Sebestiana.

24.

Where are St. John the Baptist
and our Lord going? They're
waiting for their patience
to lead them to heaven.

25.

Where is the Lord baby going?
Going with his purple tunic
and his crown of thorns and
the blood on his shoulders.

26.

They're taking him through the
street of bitterness, His feet and
hands tied, living his people.

27

Es tan estrecha la cama
Que tuvo el Hijo del hombre.
que para morir en ella
Un pie sobre él, harto pone...

28.

El domingo servio al cielo
¡Amén Jesús! le gritaban
está su mamá con Dios
Comadre Sebestiana...

Amen

27.

His bed is so narrow that son of
the man in order to die in it had
to put one foot over the other.

28.

On Sunday, He rose to
Heaven. Amen, Jesus, they
shouted. His mother is with
him comadre Sebestiana.

Amen.

President John F. Kennedy

By Enrique Chacón

1.

Editores de papeles yo les
pido frente a frente
Publícame esta desgrana
De la muerto el presidente…

2.

La bandera fue estampada con
Sangre de nuestra vena
un desastrado asesino
Vino a manchar la bandera…

3.

Esta desgracia paso a quién
devorar mis quejas esta es la
Cuidad de Dallas
Que es el estado de Tejas…

4.

Esta caso sucedió y es
tan grande maravilla
Mataron El Presidente Kennedy.
Como a las doce del día
este asesino cumplió de
veras lo que quiera…

5.

El fínate dos de Noviembre
que di a tan sin alado
Mataron al presidente un
asesino malvado…

6.

El asesino arrojo de este
edificio un balazo pues
Con la ansía de su muerte solo
se arroyo en su balazos…

1.

Newspaper Editors, I ask
you, face to face, that you
publish this disgrace, the
death of the President…

2.

The flag was stamped with
the blood of our veins; a
disastrous assassin came
to stain our banner…

3.

This disgrace happened, To whom
shall I complain, The city of
Dallas, In the state of Texas…

4.

This disgrace occurred, and it's a
great wonder, President Kennedy
was killed around 12 o'clock noon.
The assassin really accomplished
what he set out to do…

5.

The 22nd day of November; what a
day without warning. An assassin
maliciously killed the President…

6.

The bold assassin, from a
building, discharged a bullet.
With the anxiety of the
murder, he found himself in
the fuzziness of the deed…

7.

Solo se arroyo en sus por que
esta era querer El presidente caí
muerto en su brazos de su mujer
Te acaba tez vida mi a
te valiere haber…

7.

He rocked himself in the arms
of his wife; this was his love, The
President died in the arms of his
wife. You are gone Love of my
life, I'll never see you again…

8.

El asesino quería a matar al
gobernó por un descargo de la
armada lo quería con honor…

8.

The assassin wanted to kill the
governor with one discharge of
his weapon; He felt it honorable.

9.

El asesino quería a una medalla
de honor ya matado al Presidente
ya huido al gobernador
Váyame Dios de los cielos
que asesino tan traidor…

9.

The assassin wanted the Medal of
honor, He had killed the President;
He had injured the Governor.
Oh my God, from the heavens
above, what a traitorous assassin.

10.

El Asesino salió aquí como
pues a criminal ha matado al
Presidente este cobarde fatal…

10.

The assassin fled from the building,
a criminal who had murdered the
President; This deadly coward…

11.

Del delito que tenía como pues
a criminal en contra una policía
tan buen lo pudo matar…

11.

In his confusion of having
committed a crime, he fled; He
encountered a policeman; He
was able to kill him too…

12.

Lo agarran en un trato lo
llevan al pueblo hall
Lo ponen tras de las barras
para a fiarnos a lo majar…

12.

They seized him in a theater;
they're taking him to City
Hall. They put him bars. For
better security, no doubt…

13.

Lo sacan del pueblo hall al asesino
malvado con guías esposas lleva
a la cárcel del condado…

13.

They took him out of city
hall, the wicked assassin, In
handcuffs; they're taking
him to the county jail…

14.

El que mato a la asesino su nombre
no se decir tal vez eran de las
mismas y muerto no has decir...

15.

Le dicen los oficiales que cosa
indecente no teniendo mas achaque
por que mato El Presidente...

16.

Dijo todita la gente en esto
particular que un día truenan las
palos sea acordaran del peral,
Todo el mundo mirar a de
esta muerto tan fatal...

17.

Nuestro dijo presidente hizo
viaje a Dallas, Tejas
Hablar de las Bill White y
fueron vamos sus quejas...

18.

El Embajador Stevenson le dice a
si al Presidente mira no vallas allá
Que es ley de mala gente...

19.

Al embajador Stevenson en Dallas
no lo quiso una mujer desgarrada
La cara así le escupieron
mira no vallas allá te digo
por que te quiero...

14.

The one that killed the assassin;
I can't pronounce his name.
Who knows? He might have
been a co-conspirator and
dead men don't talk...

15.

The officials are saying, what
an indecent thing to do; He
has no excuse as to why he
killed the president...

16.

The people have expressed
about this tragedy that one day
a thunderous shot exploded to
change history; They will recall
the danger that day; they will
look at this a day of infamy...

17.

Our own dignified President
made a trip to Dallas, Texas, to
talk about the Bill of Rights.
His efforts were in vain...

18.

Ambassador Stevenson warned
the President, "Don't go to
Dallas, It's a lawless city."

19.

Ambassador Stevenson met a
disturbed woman in Dallas; The
woman spit in his face. Don't
go to Dallas she warned; "I
tell you because I like you."

20.

El Presidente hizo viaje en esto
particular pues ha estado de Tejas
Sin saber que iba a pasar
allí se encontró su muerto
de un asesino fatal…

20.

The President made plans for
the trip to Dallas; He couldn't
know what was to happen;
He met his death at the hands
of an infamous assassin…

21.

Pues La Señora Kennedy siento
mucho su pesar por la muerte de
su esposo de un asesino fatal…

21.

Mrs. Kennedy, I'm sorry for your
loss, for the death of your husband.
At the hands of an assassin…

22.

Gente de todo estados en esto
particular vieron a acompáñala
En el dicho funeral y
era el jefe la nación
Muy cumplido y muy legal…

22.

People from all status of life
came to accompany him at his
funeral. The head of the nation,
very complete and very honest…

23.

Lyndon Johnson es nuestro
nuevo Presidente de bajo de esto
bandera para resaber poblemos
es su tierra y en la ajena…

23.

Lyndon Jonson is our new
President; Under our flag,
to resolve problems at
home and abroad…

24.

El pueblo ha
Queda marrada la historia
Kennedy El Presidente, de
un asesino malvado que
lo mato redepente…

24.

The Nation has given him the
trust to lead; He is an educated
wise man and now he is President
of the United Status…

25.

Presidente Hablando mucha
calma yo voy hacer lo que puede
pues si todos me respaldan
queda narrada la estaña del
Presidente de un asesino malvado
que lo mato redepente…

25.

The President, speaking with calm,
status that he will do what he can;
He will need everyone's support…

26.

Lyndon Johnson esta viejo y
siempre a sido amado y ahora es el
Presidente viejo pero no apolillado!

26.

Lyndon Jonson may be old;
he's always been loved. He may
be old but not moth-eaten!

27.

El que ha trabado el careado
no siendo muy bien autor soy
de Brighton, Colorado
Yo soy El Henry
585 north 6th
Brighton, Colorado...

27.

The author, Henry (Enrique)
Chacon humbles himself by saying
he is a tongue-tied writer, meaning
that his vocabulary is limited.
I am Henry from
585 north 6th
Brighton, Colorado...

Noted: On the contrary, he
wrote it in his native tongue,
Spanish, and in poetic form
and used words that described
the tragedy very accurately and
therefore left a diary of that day
in history. The story flows much
better in Spanish. Some of the
flow is lost in translation.

Beatrice Apodaca-Montoya,
granddaughter of Henry
Chacon translated this poem
and is extremely proud of all
of Grandpa's writings. Thank
you for the privilege.

Final Words

Mom, this is your legacy it is filled with so much, to be proud of. Your history is so valuable. The people of your lineage have created Colorado History, at its finest. This alone is enough to tell the world that you are of nobility. That same nobility runs through the veins of all your children and grandchildren. We too can now see our heritage through the stories of our ancestors. Be proud of who you are. God made you special. You are my Mom.

CPSIA information can be obtained
at www.ICGtesting.com
Printed in the USA
LVHW03s0003200618
581338LV00001B/137/P

9 781456 727376